# Dancing Histories

# Dancing Histories

Heuristic Ethnography
with the Ohafia Igbo

*John C. McCall*

*Ann Arbor*

THE UNIVERSITY OF MICHIGAN PRESS

Copyright © by the University of Michigan 2000
All rights reserved
Published in the United States of America by
The University of Michigan Press
Manufactured in the United States of America
♾ Printed on acid-free paper

2003   2002   2001   2000      4   3   2   1

*A CIP catalog record for this book is available
from the British Library.*

Library of Congress Cataloging-in-Publication Data

McCall, John C. (John Christensen)
    Dancing histories : heuristic ethnography with the Ohafia Igbo /
John C. McCall.
        p.   cm.
    Includes bibliographical references and index.
    ISBN 0-472-11070-5 (cloth : alk. paper)
    1. Igbo (African people)—History.   2. Igbo (African people)—
Rites and ceremonies.   3. Philosophy, Igbo.   4. Ohafia (Nigeria)—
History.   5. Ohafia (Nigeria)—Social life and customs.
I. Title.
DT515.45.I33 M39   1999
966.9'00496332—dc21                                           99-059065

For Ibe Nwosu Kalu and his ancestors,
*Mkpukpu nne kpụrụ anagị afa nwa ya isi.*

# Contents

# Illustrations

# Acknowledgments

The question of authorship is becoming increasingly problematized. In anthropology, issues regarding "ethnography authority" (Clifford 1988:21) range from examination of the literary conventions with which we construct it, to the institutional arrangements that confer and legitimate it. In conjunction with this, the ethnographer's presentation of and dependence upon "informant authority" (46) has drawn attention to the complex exchange of minds that produces ethnographic knowledge. This complexity is effaced and distorted by the notion of authorship. While I accept full responsibility for the presentation of experiences, ideas, and understandings in the following pages, the credit must be shared. This book is a product of countless interactions and exchanges with friends, colleagues, and teachers in Ohafia, Nsukka, Bloomington, Carbondale, Cambridge, and elsewhere. I must certainly include among my collaborators the intellectual predecessors whose perspectives and insights I have encountered in classrooms, texts, proverbs, and ritual interactions in the course of my research. As author, I act as the common synthesizing nexus in this process. Nevertheless, the extent to which these endeavors fairly represent life in Ohafia is a measure of my collaborators' success in guiding me beyond my own assumptions toward a broader perspective. This process of interaction, participation in daily life, careful observation, discussion, debate, and reflection is generally glossed as "research."

Financial support for the research activities that made this book possible came from a number of generous institutions. The U.S. Department of Education provided a series of Foreign Language Area Studies Fellowships that supported my study of Igbo language as well as part of the subsequent research write-up. My initial trip to Ohafia in 1989 was funded by a Sigma Xi Grant-in-Aid of Research and a David Skomp Research Grant from the Indiana University Department of Anthropology. My second research stint in 1990–91 was made possible by a Fulbright-Hays Dissertation Research Grant. Research with the papers of G. I. Jones at the University of Cambridge in 1996 was supported by a grant from the Chicago Branch of the English-Speaking Union, a Summer Research Fellowship from Southern Illinois University, Carbondale, and a Visiting Researcher appointment provided by the University of Cambridge African Studies Centre.

Parts of this book are revised from previously published essays. "Discovery as a Research Strategy," which appeared as a commentary in the *Anthropology Newsletter* 37, no. 2 (1996): 42, 44, is included in rewritten form as a part of chapter 1. A short version of chapter 2 appeared under the same title in *Anthropology and Humanism Quarterly* 18, no. 2 (1993): 56–66. Chapter 6 is a slightly revised version of an essay by the same title that appeared in *American Anthropologist* 98, no. 1 (1996): 127–36. These three works are reprinted by permission of the American Anthropological Association. A section of chapter 3 appeared originally as part of "Dancing the Past: Experiencing Historical Knowledge in Ohafia, Nigeria," published in *Passages: A Chronical of the Humanities* 4, no. 1 (1993): 8–9, a publication of the Northwestern University Program of African Studies. Chapter 4 is slightly revised from an essay originally published under the same title in *Africa* 65, no. 2 (1995): 256–70, the journal of the International African Institute.

The individuals at Indiana University who provided intellectual guidance and practical support for this project are many. Paula Girshick, my doctoral adviser, deserves particular recognition for her steadfast encouragement and her resolute insistence that I address the most difficult questions my research raised. Like a trickster, Michael Jackson appeared in Bloomington at exactly that moment when I was ready for what he had to offer, and his guidance and scholarship have had a profound impression on my work. My gratitude goes to Michael Herzfeld who consistently supported my endeavors and who taught me to always seek the deeper question behind the apparent one. Ruth Stone and Patrick O'Meara saw me through various trials of my research and guided me on the professional ropes including grant proposals and publications. To Keith Hart, Rory Turner, J. A. K. Njoku, Susanne Lundin, and Sarah Pike, I

offer my gratitude for their cogent advice and intellectual compan-
ionship, which in various ways contributed to the formulation of
this book.

Peer reviewers who provided constructive criticism for revisions
at various stages of the writing include Alma Gottlieb, Edith Turner,
Simon Ottenberg, and Paul Stoller. Paul Stoller deserves particular
recognition for pushing me to realize the full potential of my arguments. My heartfelt gratitude goes to the late G. I. Jones, whom I
was fortunate to meet in Cambridge in 1989. His pioneering work
in Igboland in general, and Ohafia in particular, paved the way for
my own studies. Jones's scholarly concern for Igbo history and arts
and his informed critique of the colonial project at a time when his
colleagues remained enthralled with ahistorical functionalist models distinguish him as an honored intellectual ancestor. I also want
to thank Ursula Jones, who provided gracious hospitality in Cambridge and insightful stories about Jones's work in Igboland. Several
outstanding individuals at the University of Nigeria-Nsukka helped
to make my research in Nigeria productive and successful. The late
Professor O. Ndubuisi must receive special recognition for his inex-
haustible hospitality and his practical support in times of need. As
my local adviser, Professor Azuka Dike extended hospitality and
professional advice and steered me through the institutional aspects of conducting research in Nigeria. A special debt of gratitude
is owed to Professor Chukwuma Azuonye who helped me to make
sense of some particularly troublesome texts in Ohafia dialect and
whose studies and transcriptions of Ohafia oratory have greatly
enhanced my own work. Professor C. O. C. Agwu deserves thanks
for providing botanical identifications.

The debt of gratitude that I owe to the people of Ohafia is immea-
surable. Chief and Madam Ukwa made my family and me feel at
home in our house in Amaekpu. Justice Agwu Kalu and his family
provided friendship and good counsel. His Royal Highness Udumeze
Eze O. Uma freely shared his detailed knowledge of Ohafia history
and culture and opened many possibilities for my research. The
people of the town of Akanu helped me in innumerable ways. Special recognition is due to Nne Uko Uma Awa, to whose life I have
seen fit to devote a full chapter. To the many people who graciously

spent their time allowing me to interview them and record their music I offer heartfelt thanks. To my assistant John Ajike Kalu Ume who appears herein as "Jakus" I owe many thanks for his time, efforts, and insights, as well as those of his departed father Ajike K. Ume whose writings provide a unique and rich view of Ohafia's past. Joseph Agara taught me nearly everything that I know about Ohafia music and dance. His cogent analysis of Ohafia culture profoundly shaped my own and is reflected throughout this book.

My parents, who assisted this project in innumerable ways, have my profound thanks. To my sons Ian and Robin McCall, who weathered long separations from family and friends, and who helped to establish my own worth in Ohafia as a man with two fine sons, I offer my heartfelt thanks. To my wife, Clare McCall, who encouraged my dream of becoming an anthropologist, who kept me going through the most discouraging phases of my work, who pored over the drafts for this book as many times as I, and who has always been my most constructive critic and astute literary adviser, I owe lifelong gratitude. The debt that I owe Ibe Nwosu Kalu is inestimable. An erudite scholar in his own right, he appears on these pages as he does in life, as Mr. Ink. Titles such as research assistant and translator pale next to the immense contribution that Ink made to this work. Collaborator, colleague, co-conspiritor, kindred spirit, come closer. His ability to forge links between his own extensive knowledge of Ohafia culture and my peculiar intellectual goals makes this book what it is. I am honored to call him *nwa nna* (brother) and accept the responsibilities that term implies. To Ink and his family, who made me one of their own, I dedicate this book.

# PART 1

# Heuristic Ethnography

Perhaps this [African] gnosis makes more sense if seen as a result of two processes: first, a permanent reevaluation of the limits of anthropology as knowledge in order to transform it into a more credible *anthropou-logos,* that is a discourse on a human being; and, second, an examination of its own historicity.

(Mudimbe 1988:186)

. . . there is something else to which we are witness, and which we might describe as an *insurrection of subjugated knowledges.*

(Foucault 1980:81, italics in original)

CHAPTER 1

# Outline of a Method

I was well into my field research in Ohafia, Nigeria, before I fully appreciated the importance of the war dance to my research. By then I had seen the dance performed during many burial ceremonies and other events. I had recordings of the music and a video of war dancers performing at the New Yam festival. I had conducted numerous interviews with people about the war dance and I felt I had plenty of "data" on the genre. I had not, however, interviewed any musicians. So I was pleased when my friend Ink told me that a renowned drummer named Oke Mmuko wanted to speak to me.

It was evening when we strolled down the path into Utugokoko Akanu to find Chief Oke. Darkness was enveloping the village, and the path through the night market was lined with kerosene lamps, each casting a small pool of illumination on fruits, dried fish, greens, and other goods. When we arrived at the Utugokoko meetinghouse (*obu*), an informal gathering of the Ekpe men's society had begun in the neighboring compound. A tape of Ekpe music recorded at a recent burial was playing on a portable cassette player, and *kaikai* and palm wine flowed freely.[1] This was not a *true* meeting of Ekpe; such meetings require certain formalities and the retrieval of the official instruments from the shrine. However, the sound of recorded Ekpe music engendered the spirit that "Ekpe was on," and members were gathering, moving, and greeting in the idiosyncratic style of the secret society: gestures that they would otherwise avoid in the course of mundane interaction.

An Ekpe man himself, Chief Oke was among the revelers, and we called him aside to arrange the interview. Various men began to join the discussion, and soon a small crowd had gathered on the veranda in front of the meetinghouse. An argument ensued regarding who should participate in the interview. As the stridency of voices increased I quickly became frustrated by the turn that the negotiations had taken. My plans to interview individuals often expanded to include an assembly of self-appointed "experts" all of whom expected to eat and drink to their heart's content. Ink, always a defender of my pocketbook, was haggling with them, and no one seemed interested in my opinion regarding the matter.

Escaping the negotiations for a moment, I retreated to the corner of the veranda and watched the Ekpe men next door. Using this opportunity to increase my own repertoire of secret signs, I observed them as they challenged each other with the arcane gestures.[2] Soon Ink approached me asking why I had left the discussion. I grumbled something, and he explained that he had successfully dissuaded the extraneous participants but that Chief Oke wanted the assistance of three percussionists, a young singer, and a dancer. I protested: "I just want to talk to him! I'm not asking for a performance." Ink gave a puzzled expression that I had come to know meant that I needed to stop being thickheaded, so I assented to the arrangements and we returned to Ink's compound. Chief Oke had said that he would come in about an hour. But it was midnight before the assembly of performers hiked up the hill. By this time I was exhausted. I felt the whole event had slipped out of my control, and that I might not be able to structure the interview to address the questions that I considered pertinent to my research.

The sky was moonless and clear. A single kerosene lamp sat on a small table casting a dim circle of light across the sandy yard. Chief Oke and his accompanists sat on a bench next to the chairs where Ink and I sat. We shared kola, and Chief Oke began immediately with traditional oratorical greetings and then recounted the legend of the origin of the war dance.

Since Ohafia people were very brave and were known as warriors, other villages would hire them to wage war with their enemies. When they went, they conquered and came home with trophy heads. When you went with others to war and returned with a head you felt very proud. That sense of belonging, that you were a man, kept you happy. But in those early days it was not yet known how to celebrate the heads. In those days there was a woman from Ebem. Her first son went with others to war and he did not come back. Her second son, when he came of age also went to war, and like his brother, he did not return. Then this woman had a third son named Egbelenwa. He was not allowed to join other boys. She dressed him as a girl and he played with girls. She didn't want this son to go to war. Egbelenwa never knew that he was a boy, but when he grew up his age mates saw that he was a man and without telling his mother they took him with them to war. As God would have it, he came home with a head. As he returned and passed through the first Ohafia village some of his relatives saw him and recognized him. They killed a goat for him. As he was traveling on, news reached his mother that Egbelenwa was coming, and that he was being carried shoulder high with the head he had taken. When the mother heard this her heart was full of joy. When he reached home she bought clothes to dress him as a warrior. She was so proud that she announced to the village that her son's bravery must be celebrated. She purchased a goat and killed it and she bought many chickens for the feast. The men decided that they must create a dance to be used in celebration. They said that they must have a war dance. So they cut sticks to produce music and they made a song. (Mmuko 1991)

At this point in the story the percussionists began to play the distinctive rhythm of the war dance using the bamboo slats known as *akwatankwa,* and Chief Oke sang, the other men joining in an ostinato chorus:

Egbelenwa wụ ugo (Egbelenwa is an eagle)
Aa-ah, Egbelenwa wụ ugo
Aa-ah ya, Egbelenwa wụ ugo
Aa-ah yo, Egbelenwa wụ ugo
Oo-oh ya, Egbelenwa wụ ugo

They sang that Egbelenwa was an eagle. They put a leopard cap on his head to show that he was a strong man and an eagle feather in the cap to indicate that he was a warrior. That is how the war dance started. (Mmuko 1991)[3]

I had hoped that Chief Oke would explain the significance of *ọfụfụ*—a distinctive feature of the dance characterized by rippling undulations of the pectoral muscles causing the entire chest to pulsate continuously. I knew that ọfụfụ was associated with the ancestral legacy of warriorhood. Its occurrence marks the peak of a performance, or, in the evocative language of Igbo metaphor: "when the music takes fire, the flesh melts." But when I asked about ọfụfụ Oke seemed puzzled. He stated what happened to him to be obvious: "Ọfụfụ is associated with strength, to show the smartness of running to war, getting a head and then running back." Ink laughed and said, "It's a dry subject." I had hoped for more exegesis—a symbolic interpretation—but I began to realize that my plans for the interview were misguided. Chief Oke wanted to teach me about the war dance in his own way, in the way that knowledge about the dance has always been shared. As if sensing my realization, Chief Oke struck his drum signaling the vocalist to come forward. He took a shot glass full of gin and, while slowly dripping the liquid on the ground, moved gracefully about the yard calling Ink's ancestors to join the festivities.

> Ibe-a Kamalu come drink wine!
> Ikpang the Great come drink wine!
> Okwun Ibe Aja come and share my wine!
> Call great father Omezue Uwa to come quickly!
> The force encountered in the forest is death!
> Odo Awa the great come and share my drink!
> Ibe Imaga drink wine!
> Umachi Ajike, himself a warrior, advance, we drink here!
> Land of Ohafia Ezema,
> He who goes farm yams should return!
> The one who goes to tap wine should return!
> The hunter should return!
> If the war is uncertain, still none will run away![4]

Then he shouted, "Ndi Ibe *kwe nụ!*" and all responded with approval. The percussionists began playing again, and Chief Oke struck a command in the language of the drum. A young man who had been standing at the periphery moved swiftly to the center. The glow of the lantern seemed to cling to his gleaming form as he began the mincing movements of the dance.

I had seen the war dance countless times before but I had never witnessed anything like what I then beheld. The dance was narrative, telling a story of travel and conquest. The man moved across the ground with actions so exact and subtle that they had an aura of invisibility about them. The combination of ridged bodily tension and fluid ease of motion that this man exhibited resembled the stealthy prowl of a leopard moving in for a kill. As the dance unfolded I realized that beyond the faint sphere of light cast by the lamp a crowd of people huddled, watching this extraordinary performance. I have no idea how much time passed as I fell under the spell of the dancer's narrative. When the musicians "set fire to the music" the dancer performed, in mimesis, the quintessential act of realized Ohafia manhood: swinging an invisible cutlass, he decapitated his imaginary foe, securing his trophy in a bag at his waist. Pantomime yes, but so compellingly performed that it evoked in me a visceral sense of the fear and awe that Ohafia warriors have always inspired. The dance continued into the night. My fatigue had disappeared, and I sat captivated by the performance until, at length, parting words were exchanged, and the small band of musicians meandered down the hill and back into the sleeping village.

I remained for some time in the starlit yard reflecting on what had transpired. These brilliant performers had shown me more than a war dance. They had demonstrated the limits of my received concept of what constituted meaningful "data" for my research. I wanted to interview them *about* the war dance but they insisted that I *see* and *hear* the dance. I thought I had already "seen" the dance, but what was presented to me that night was quite distinct from the performances I had recorded at burials and festivals. In the wake of that powerfully evocative dance, I reflected on the limits of discursive expressions of knowledge. To know the war dance was to experience it again and again in differing contexts: in honor of your brother's completion of a university degree; at your father's burial. To truly understand the dance was to know the hope that it would someday be performed in celebration of one's own accomplishments. The performance of the war dance creates a link to the past in that it includes the participants and particularly those honored by it as an acknowledged part of the grand continuum of history. I realized at last that these performative acts constitute an order of knowledge that is qualitatively distinct from discursive formulations.

History that is danced produces a knowledge of the past that is more, or rather, other than a mere narrative. As an embodied act it makes reference to the past as an embodied experience—and this reference is captured as a nonverbal aesthetic *abstraction.* The classic debates on the subject of "African thought" (Evans-Pritchard 1937, 1956; Fortes 1959; Fortes and Dieterlen 1965; Horton 1967, 1970; Mbiti 1969; Griaule 1965; Calame-Griaule 1965; and later Mudimbe 1988; Appiah 1992; and many others) address the problem with an assumption that knowledge is linguistically constituted. The language-based model of cognition, taken to an extreme in structuralism and deconstruction, has led anthropologists to study nonlinguistic phenomena—dance, music, architecture, artifacts, and even culture itself—*as* texts. While not denying the utility of many of these studies I am attempting something different here. In asking the question "what does it mean to dance history?" I do not intend to divine a historical "text" implicit in the dance. I want to explore what it means to know history by way of dance. Following this logic further, I want to discover what it means to understand society by way of embodied existence in the context of particular sociocultural and historical circumstances. Finally, I want to examine where this pursuit leads in terms of possible alternative epistemologies of social and historical knowledge.


**Toward Objectivity**


What I undertake here is not a dance. It is a book. Embodied knowledge and discursive knowledge are not directly and simply commensurable but neither are they hopelessly incommensurable. The representation of embodied and experiential knowledge requires a manner of writing that applies the full power of literary tools to the scientific project. The raw material of the human sciences is experiential, and our discursive formulations—stories, poems, ethnographies— are successful in transmitting that knowledge to the extent that they render human experience in a nuanced and evocative manner. The basic anthropological fact that different people objectify the world in diverse ways and that human objectifications are both constituted by and constitutive of social processes suggests that anthropology holds a unique position to explore the epistemological grounds of knowledge. Accepting anthropology's maxim that people endowed with different cultural resources objectify the world in radically different ways and by different means—and that scientists are in no way exempt from this process—does not necessarily lead to a solipsistic claim that no "objective" world exists, or that one truth is always just as good as any other. And I think very few anthropologists assume this. This recognition of the researcher as inextricably *within* the complex play of cultural knowledges is crucial if we are to overcome the limits of our own subjectivities to understand the subjectivities of others. Framing objectivity in this manner moves emphasis away from a naïve and reified notion of objectivity toward a focus on the underlying problem of objectification—those socially informed processes by which we structure experiences in a manner that imbues them with coherence and meaning.

I suggest there is a cluster of methodologies emerging in anthropology that constitutes what I call a heuristic approach to ethnography. Some aspects of this approach—emphasis on ongoing cultural participation, methodological relativism, and careful exegesis of indigenous views of the world—are the legacy of modern anthropology with roots in the seminal works of recognized founders such as Boas, Malinowski, and Griaule. Heuristic methods as I frame them here, however, emerged fully only when the concept of isolated cultural islands constructed by functionalist theory was abandoned beginning in the 1960s. Going back at least to Spencer (1860, 1885) the functional model of a closed internally coherent cultural system had tremendous utility for anthropological relativism, but the circular

logic and ahistoricity of functionalism proved inadequate to sustain
inquiry in the postcolonial era. As Fabian cogently noted:

> Once other cultures are fenced off as cultural gardens or, in the
> terminology of sociological jargon, as boundary-maintaining sys-
> tems based on shared values; once each culture is perceived as
> living its Time, it becomes possible and indeed necessary to ele-
> vate the interstices between cultures to a methodological status.
> At that moment the study of cultures "from a distance," clearly a
> vice in terms of the injunction demanding empirical research
> through participant observation, may turn into a theoretical vir-
> tue. A situation of political antagonism may then be rationalized
> epistemologically as the kind of objective distance that allows the
> anthropologist to view another culture in its entirety. (1983:47)

In the wake of functionalism's demise a wave of new approaches
glossed by Marcus and Fisher (1984) as an "experimental moment"
has characterized recent anthropological research practices. Some of
these researchers (Apter 1992; Feld 1982; Gottlieb 1992; Jackson 1982,
1989; Stoller 1989b, 1997; Turner 1992; to name but a few) approach
their work heuristically—they treat indigenous models as theories
rather than as data. The new heuristic ethnographies are often classi-
fied as "postmodernist" and carelessly lumped together with studies
that analyze ethnography as a genre of literature drawing theoretical
insights from poststructural literary criticism and Frankfurt school
critical theory. While all these approaches share a critical thrust and a
suspicion of the colonial assumptions undergirding structuralist and
functionalist models, heuristic ethnographies distinguish themselves
by their commitment to fieldwork as the foundation of anthropological research. Unlike text criticism, heuristic research is, in many ways,
a fulfillment of, rather than a break from, the empirical ethnographic
traditions pioneered by Boas, Malinowski, and Griaule.

Heuristic methodologies in anthropology provide a unique opportunity to go beyond recent intellectual exercises in which we use
critical theory to deconstruct academic objectifications. They provide
new and sometimes unexpected answers to the questions left hang-
ing by critical theory and poststructural analysis. By engaging the

possibility of thinking otherwise—objectifying our experiences on different terms—we are better able to reflect upon our acquired habits of perception, interpretation, and objectification. This simple truth, however, continues to be obscured in the most recent manifestation of the age-old debate regarding the place of science in anthropology.

In the wake of heated debate on the subject at the 1994 annual meeting of the American Anthropological Association both in panels and at the general business meeting, the Association provided various platforms for discussion of this issue. *Anthropology Newsletter* declared "Science in Anthropology" as its annual theme for 1995–96 (Skomal 1995:3). What distresses me about the flavor of much of the ongoing debate is its limited vision of what social science is and what it is capable of becoming. In an *Anthropology Newsletter* article, Givens and Jablonski (1995:11) classify all sociocultural anthropologists into four categories: *scientists*—who are identified as antisubjective; *interpretivists*—who "prefer to speculate rather than replicate" because they "deny that objective meanings exist"; *postmodernists*—who simply "prefer subjectivity to science"; and *advocates*—who "value subjects over science." It is likely that the authors would be quick to assign the various approaches that I have referred to as experiential anthropology to one or more of their subjectivist, antiobjective, antiscience categories. I, however, want to go on record as rejecting any effort to exile myself and my colleagues from the halls of social science.

I am reminded of Hayden White's (1978:27–29) cogent discussion of a parallel "science vs. humanities" debate in the discipline of history. White observes that while historians claim to form a bridge between the arts and sciences, they have often failed to keep up with either and tend to remain locked into what are essentially nineteenth-century conceptions of both—complete with the Victorian notion that science and art are somehow fundamentally opposed to one another. I feel that the same can be said of the current debates in anthropology. What is missing from arguments framed in terms of these dichotomies of science and art, object and subject, is that the people we study, unlike the objects of physics and chemistry, are thinking, theorizing subjects in their own right.

This fact is not a problem that requires some sort of "distancing" methodology. It is the most valuable resource we have for learning how to theorize about the social. If ethnography is to be an "objective" science capable of addressing questions of motivation, agency, and meaning, we must be able to surpass the subjectivity of our own received knowledge. We are hindered by the assumption that the trajectory of European intellectual history constitutes an exclusive path to objective truth. I suggest that we can find valuable perspectives in the insights shared with us by the people we study. Objectivity in this formulation is not something we bring to our research. It is something we discover through the process of engaging in day-to-day life and establishing an open-minded dialogue and exchange of ideas with the people whose lives we study. This is the notion of objectivity that John Chernoff (1979:10) refers to when he writes of his field research in Ghana, "my 'objectivity' is what I was when I was there, that part of Africa which I became, a fact in the lives and minds of those who knew me."

My point is this: the indigenous understandings of the world that we gain knowledge of through field research do not merely provide data for analysis. They can, and must, be mobilized as a source of theoretical insights. This is no easy task. Serious epistemological issues must be confronted and addressed with critical imagination. It is no longer enough to identify a function or structure of a particular way of knowing the world. We must now attempt to come to terms with what it means to live in the world such knowledge constitutes. Heuristic approaches in anthropology provide a means to apply the knowledge of the world that we gain through dialogue with other peoples to perennial questions of human existence— questions that have been addressed in various ways by people in every society. It moves anthropology from studying *about* other people to studying *with* other people.

## Heuristic Ethnography

Marcus and Fisher (1986) identified a "crisis of representation" more than a decade ago. Since then it has become clear that cultural anthropology has entered a phase of intellectual uncertainty. The debates that engage us, revolving around dichotomies of science and humanism, structure and agency, materialism and idealism, are decidedly lacking in scholarly fervor. They are not animated by the potential emergence of a new synthesis but have a sense of desperation about them—as if we are attempting to stir flames from the coals of a dying fire. Some anthropologists have voiced fears that ethnography—conceived in an era of colonial expansion—may not be able to survive the collapse of modernist paradigms. If we can distill any conclusive wisdom from these debates, it is that anthropology appears to have become "postparadigmatic." We may never again be able to define our discipline in terms of shared goals, commonly held models of society, and consensus regarding the relevant questions to address. It has become commonplace to argue that we can no longer depend on master narratives, essentialist models, and programmatic paradigms to structure our discourse. But the question remains: is it still relevant and productive to conduct rigorous research with a systematic methodology? I argue that it is. I propose that ethnography will not only survive this crisis but will provide solutions to the seemingly intractable question of how to conceptualize the postparadigmatic human sciences.

In the absence of a structuring paradigm, anthropologists have developed a critical reflexivity regarding the conditions and relations of research and how these shape our ethnographic analyses. We have begun to make room for indigenous voices in our representations. Faced with the necessity to find coherence in the complex experiential data produced by field research, and wary of top-down theorizing, anthropologists are beginning to take indigenous views more seriously than ever before. Whether working with farmers in Mexico, homeless people in Philadelphia, or prostitutes in Bombay, anthropologists have always considered the poignant ways in which people meet the conditions that shape their lives a compelling justification for the relevance of anthropological inquiry. What is pertinent about the present situation is that the theoretical vacuum at the top has created a new valence for the ideas we encounter on the ground.

## From Data to Theory

We are on the cusp of a profound change in our conception of the relationship between theory and data in the social sciences. As skepticism grows regarding "ethnographic authority" and constructions of the "Ethnographic Other," anthropologists are increasingly willing to listen seriously to what the people they study have to say about the societies they live in. Applied anthropologists are ahead of the game in this, having long noted that indigenous people often have superior theoretical understandings of their local ecosystems— even if the cosmological and symbolic idioms of this knowledge are difficult for academic ecologists to understand and accept. But this type of realization is now becoming relevant to sociocultural anthropologists in general. With the present ambivalence toward the theoretical options available to researchers, why shouldn't the concepts of the social world held by the people who are being studied be allowed to compete on equal terms in the theoretical discourse?

Traditionally the utterances of our "informants" were data, pure and simple. Theory was something the anthropologist brought from without and applied to the data. The final result, if all went well, was an explanatory model. This neat division of knowledges into categories designating that "their" knowledge produces data and "our" knowledge produces theory has a decidedly colonial configuration. Nevertheless, the assumption that academic theorization has an exclusive claim to the status of objective metaknowledge has been remarkably persistent. This intellectual apartheid has prevented the ideas of the people we study from entering the walled neighborhoods of academic discourse without a pass—an "ethno-" prefix as in "ethnophilosophy," "ethnopharmacology," and so on, designating these conceptions as "data."

The goal of anthropology must not be to claim a privileged view of others, but rather to form a bridge between our rationalities and theirs. The naïve notion that the privilege of objectivity is the legacy of the intellectual descendants of the European Enlightenment is now giving way to a focus on the problem of objectification—what are the practices, instrumental arrangements, and rationalities employed by people as they objectify their worlds? This concern draws our attention to the practical social theories mobilized by people in everyday life. As we strive to take our analyses beyond basic explanations of functional structures or cognitive rules, we are finding that the people we study are quite capable of contributing new perspectives to the problem-solving project in which we are engaged. The question is one of translation, and not just in the simple linguistic sense. In reflecting upon my own research process as well as examining the work of other anthropologists who are conducting heuristic research, certain common methods for bridging epistemic gaps become apparent. These are rarely made explicit, but I think it is useful to identify specific methodological strategies that characterize the most rigorously conducted examples of heuristic research. The discussion below is not presented as a prescription for an "ideal" research program but rather as an outline of my research process, which will assist the reader in understanding this book as well as an emerging methodology in ethnography that is rarely analyzed systematically.

## Method in Heuristic Ethnography

### 1.　*Discovering Concepts On the Ground*

Heuristic ethnography is a *radically inductive* method that begins with the assumption that the ideas operative on the ground in a given society constitute a body of indigenous social theories in and of themselves. It is important to distinguish *radical induction* from methodological or logical induction, which develops general theoretical principles on the basis of formal characteristics of the data accumulated. By *radically inductive,* I mean that the putative boundary between data and theory becomes permeable in both directions. In other words, the concepts, metaphors, behavioral patterns, and practical knowledge that people employ to explain and cope with their social worlds are treated as theoretical constructs with an explanatory potential *equivalent* to those ideas we derive from the repertoire of academic knowledge we call social theory.

　　This is not to say that we should simply accept people's views of their worlds as valid. Indigenous conceptions must be subjected to the same critical strictures we apply to other analytical tools— but not before their full explanatory potential has been explored through careful exegesis. This step is the most crucial and challenging phase of the analysis. One problem that arises is that indigenous conceptions of the world are often framed in idioms, metaphors, and ritual practices that can lead the external observer to interpret the knowledge that informs them as "irrational" or concerned with "supernatural" phenomena. Thus, the practical rationality of these perspectives is often lost in translation. Therefore, the first step in heuristic ethnography is to conduct scrupulous field research with a focus on "thick description" and detailed critical hermeneutics. The objective is to go beyond reified models of "belief systems" or "ideological structures" to get at the ways in which knowledge is mobilized, reflected upon, and criticized in practice. This is done with the assumption that there is no single "culture," "mentality," or "worldview" to be captured. Knowledge is always diverse in form and characterized by complex critical tensions and compromises. It is these tensions—the points of contention, conceptual fissures, and inconsistencies—that reveal the character of discourse on the social in any community.[5]

For instance, this book concerns itself with Ohafia Igbo concepts of history. For the Igbo, masquerade dance is an important medium for representing the past and exploring the significance of ancestors. As I came to understand the instrumental theory of history embodied in Igbo masquerade performance, my investigation moved beyond a search for historical "facts," and also beyond the question of what local people "believed" about their past. The people of Ohafia taught me that history is a dance of contingent truths that are subject to continual interpretation. The dynamic and improvisatory dance of spirits embodied by masked performers frames the past as a complex, indeterminate body of knowledge. In subsequent chapters I will demonstrate that this insight is not merely an artifact of "ethnophilosophy" characteristic of a "traditional" Igbo worldview. It is a product of a dialogue with colonial and neocolonial narratives and constitutes a cogent critique of progressivist models of history.

## 2. Bridging Epistemic Gaps

When indigenous theoretical perspectives are identified, the ethnographer must seek *paradigmatic affinities* between the forms of knowledge operative on the ground in particular societies and the social theories we use in constructing explanatory models. As an Igbo masquerade dances through a village it charts a particular landscape delineating and celebrating a network of patrilocal descent groups characterized by segmentary relations. But my research revealed that the masked dance also makes reference to other histories that stand in sharp contrast to the official history of kindred community. Forced migrations, social disruptions, scandals, and tragedies are alluded to in the arcane performance through cryptic symbolic displays. In fact, these representations of the past have paradigmatic affinities in anthropological discourse. Within the official histories that recount the ancestry of descent groups and reiterate kin links that bind the community can be found the basic concepts from which structural-functional models of lineage organization were constructed. The arcane references to discontinuity, migration, and social disruption index the very materials from which critical historical models were formulated as a criticism of the structural-functional approach. What I find productive in the masquerade's representation is the relationship between these different views of the past. Rather than framing them as divergent paradigms contending for truth status they are both integral facets of the same performance. (See chapter 5 for an in-depth examination of this issue.)

Thus, identifying paradigmatic affinities provides new perspectives on familiar concepts and helps to reduce ethnography's tendency toward extreme relativism and the over-exotification of indigenous views. Mobilizing conceptual tools that derive from a synthesis of academic and ethnographic sources also facilitates the paradigmatic translation process—making our interpretations more intelligible to those in either community. Paradigmatic affinities are epistemic intersections where the possibilities for intercultural knowledge are the greatest. These affinities signal analytical perspectives with high heuristic potential.

No researcher is free of motivations and the anticipation of particular results. It is disingenuous to propose that we can approach our work from a disinterested position of pure objectivity. Thus, a reflexive awareness of the conditions that constitute our own intellectual positioning is necessary. Likewise, the interests and historical conditions that shape and motivate the people we study must also be examined critically and in depth. All of these elements come into play in the process of identifying paradigmatic affinities. The heuristic ethnographer treats these factors as initial conditions from which dialogue and intellectual exchange can originate. Paradigmatic affinities are those lines of inquiry and analysis that generate the most productive exchanges between initial positions and that allow the constitution of intermediary positions. The desired end product is a theoretical framework capable of addressing anthropological questions, one that is also consonant with the ways in which basic notions such as personhood, power, and society are objectified within the community in question.

### 3. On False Consciousness

Finally, it is important to address the problem of "false consciousness." It is a matter of common agreement among most social scientists, Marxist and otherwise, that ideological systems often function to "naturalize" and thus "normalize" social inequalities. Heuristic ethnography must address this potential argument against the validity of concepts on the ground in three ways. First, the visions of society elicited must be multiple and drawn from different sectors of society. Favoring the notions of either dominant or subjugated peoples will tend to produce incomplete, one-dimensional models.

Second, the explanations, models, analogies, and representations gained through research must be subjected to the same critical evaluation as any other theoretical perspectives derived from more conventional sources would be. We must assume that indigenous knowledges, like all knowledges, are socially situated constructs and not "objective" models of social reality.

Third, it must be emphasized that heuristic ethnography attempts to address the false consciousness that resides at the very core of the social sciences: the assumption of intellectual authority exercised by the researcher in relation to the people researched. Thus, this method is a logical consequence of the need for increased critical reflexivity in anthropological representation as we endeavor to decolonize anthropological discourse.

Heuristic ethnography moves beyond the inclusion of "other voices," toward an open exchange of ideas between the researcher and the people studied and the mobilization of indigenous rationalities in the construction of analytical tools. Such an approach requires new representational strategies. The current turn toward more literary forms of writing ethnography is a response to this need. Far from being a simple matter of style, those ethnographies that utilize detailed and often sensual description, exegetical hermeneutics, biography, storytelling, and other "writerly" methods are using these techniques to create powerful evocations of life in the communities they represent and of the experiences of people living in those communities. This representational strategy is crucial because practical knowledges are often embodied in and realized through lived experience rather than formalized discourse. Thus, the rigorous development of literary complexity in ethnography is a matter of theoretical substance rather than of style.

Heuristic methods are emerging in various forms in ethnographic presentations. The scope of heuristic experimentation in ethnographic research and writing transcends regional areas and topical specialties, so much so that any attempt to identify exemplars and enumerate, categorize, and construct a critique of approaches would constitute the subject of another project altogether. My goal here is to outline and apply a research strategy that constitutes a productive new direction in ethnography.

As the globalization of information exchange becomes the norm in the twenty-first century, the conceit of Western academic analytical privilege must give way at last to the possibility of intercultural dynamics of knowledge. Anthropologists are in a unique position in this regard because we have always been concerned with the diversity of human knowledge. If we assume an inclusive "We" and pursue a broadly heuristic exploration of the range of human knowledges, then what "We" know will prove to be a much richer body of knowledge. It is not enough to recognize that the global exchange of knowledge is increasingly becoming an attribute of the social systems we analyze. This exchange must be incorporated into the process of social analysis itself. The world is rich in epistemic diversity. There are many who have the resources to think otherwise. But we must first learn how to listen to what they have to say.

## CHAPTER 2

# Making Peace with Agwu

This is a story of an initiation ceremony and the events leading up to it. The account is autobiographical; the initiate is myself. While not strictly ethnographic, it is an account of events that are the consequence of ethnographic research. It illustrates an issue that arose for me during my research and that I think many ethnographers confront during their fieldwork: that sincere and prolonged participation in another culture can eventually challenge one's fundamental ontological assumptions. In Bronislaw Malinowski's (1922:25) classic essay on ethnographic method he declares that the "final goal, of which the Ethnographer should never lose sight . . . is . . . to grasp the native's point of view, his relation to life, to realise *his* vision of *his* world" (italics in original). If we take Malinowski's charter to heart we inevitably find it necessary to reconcile ourselves with the "world" thus realized. The so-called fictive kinship so often extended to the long-term field researcher carries with it both rights and responsibilities that are anything but fictive. The rights of kinship offer the ethnographer intimate experiences of the culture he or she seeks to understand. The responsibilities include any number of moral obligations to one's adopted kinspeople. In my own case, I found that my new family included ancestral spirits and a powerful deity named Agwu with whom I was obliged to make peace.

Positioned at the intersection between "my story" (autobiography) and "their culture" (ethnography), this account begs the question of the place of subjectivity in the production of anthropological research. Problematics in which the objective and subjective are presented as discrete "modes of knowledge" fail to comprehend the extent to which these two concepts are products of a particular categorization of the continuum of experience, a systematization mired in the agendas and personalities of Western academic history. In anthropology the subjective/objective distinction has become a shell game used to artfully avoid the ontological issues that are the inevitable result of Malinowski's charter. The term *participant observation,* which Paul Stoller (1989a:155) perceptively calls "anthropology's most famous oxymoron," embodies this sleight of hand. Michael Jackson (1989:181–82) warns against the view that "implies an absurd antinomy between objectivity and subjectivity, and the idea that we must somehow choose between one or the other." In practice the noun *objectivity* usually functions as a code word for the a priori "truth" accorded to Western academic modes of discourse. I am more interested in the verb hidden behind the noun: the processes of objectification by which experience becomes knowledge and knowledge becomes objectified. Once the notion of objectivity is disengaged from those assumptions that privilege Western ontology, one can begin to see that objectivity is a point of intersection between the world I study and the facet of that world that I become. My story begins with "dreaming the other" and ends with a rite of incorporation, a ritual of "becoming the other." It is a chronicle of a journey that originates in my experience of ontological uncertainty and leads to a process of objectification through collective social praxis.

## Dreaming the Other

It might seem that no experience should be more deserving of the label *subjective* than a dream. A dream is an internalized experience, unrestricted by the boundaries of the material world or the limitations of consequential causality. Nevertheless, dreams are socially constituted. The events, objects, and logic of dreams are framed in terms of specific cultural meanings. When, in the course of ethnographic research, one becomes immersed in another culture, one finds that one not only acquires a new language and a fragmentary understanding of an alien worldview, one also experiences an emerging sense of another reality. It is enthralling and profoundly disturbing to find oneself dreaming in a new and unfamiliar way, and to be compelled to reflect upon those dreams on their own terms.

## For Want of a Hat

Anthropologists are inveterate collectors. While I was in Ohafia I collected many things, including hats. I had a leopard hat of the type worn by Ohafia warriors, Ekpe secret society hats of both the local and Calabar varieties, and other hats of various regional types. I was fascinated by them and by the importance of hats in "wearing" one's identity. However, I felt my collection wasn't complete without the cowry shell–laden, porcupine quill–covered hat of the dibịa, the traditional doctor. It was when I began to discuss my interest in getting a dibịa hat that my friend Ink, who was a skilled dibịa himself, finally brought up the possibility of initiation. It wasn't that I needed to become an initiated dibịa to own the hat. Ink was concerned because I had been learning about the practice informally for over a year. He worried that Agwu, the spirit through whom dibịa gain their powers, might begin to "bother" me in order to compel me to undergo initiation. I had heard countless stories about members of dibịa families who had neglected their responsibility to become initiated. They experienced chronic misfortune and disease, sometimes deteriorating to complete paralysis if the obligation was ignored for too long. Eventually the unfortunate victim would seek the help of a diviner who would reveal that Agwu was behind the troubles. An initiation ceremony would be performed to make peace with Agwu and everything would be set aright. When Ink first suggested initiation I responded: "How can I? My father was not a dibịa." Ink looked at me a bit incredulously and said: "But you are my brother! You are a member of our compound."

I should have realized all along that the possibility of initiation existed for me. Although I had already sought and gained entry into the Ekpe secret society, I had assumed that the rule limiting the dibịa practice to certain patrilineages meant that I wouldn't be able to gain entry into the healer's trade. This belief was consoling because I was wary of the difficult personal and professional issue of long-term commitment that dibịa initiation would entail. Ekpe participation was largely a matter of music, dance, feasting, and camaraderie. A true commitment to dibịa would require embracing an ontology that I wasn't sure I was ready to confront. I had led myself to believe

Fig. 1.   A group of dibịa in procession wearing their quill-
and cowry-covered hats. *(Akanu Ohafia 1989)*

I could study dibịa practices and yet remain an outsider. In actuality,
the contradiction embodied in the researcher's notion of "participant observation" had become transparent.

Ink agreed to help me acquire a dibịa hat, and we left the issue of
initiation unresolved. Within a few days I went with Ink and his
junior wife Patience to the dibịa market in the city of Aba to get the
necessary supplies to construct the hat. While Ink was collecting materials for it, I collected other things. The market was vast: roots and
herbs in countless variety, displays of hundreds of dried reptiles,
birds, monkeys, and other animals, carved objects and arcane tools.
When I had first walked amid this array at market their outré other-
ness had fascinated me. By this time, though, I could gaze upon everything with the practical utility of a plumber in a hardware store. My
casual familiarity with the merchandise amused and delighted the
vendors. I filled my bag with an assortment of herbs, ritual objects,
animal parts, and other miscellany, wondering what the customs
officials would make of it all when I returned to the States.

Ink and Patience stayed in Aba, but I returned to Ohafia that evening. The bush cab was crowded, and my fellow passengers were curious about the bag of juju the American had bought at the market. As we raced along the ragged ridge-top road, dodging potholes and landslides, a panoramic expanse of bush broken by occasional garden plots spread out to the horizon in every direction. There were two Ohafia girls in the back seat who sang and clapped the whole way. As the car bounced along the road, ringing with the snappy counterpoint of the girls' voices, I couldn't help but think what an inscrutably wonderful place I was living in and how much I was going to miss it when I had to leave in just a few short weeks.

## The Night Messenger

That night I dreamt I was in my home in the village of Amaekpu. At my door appeared a handsome and distinguished African man dressed in the elegant style of a traditional chief. Though I didn't know him, I immediately felt I should trust him. I invited him in but he told me he was going to the nearby village of Ebem and asked me to join him. As we began the long walk to Ebem he suggested that we fly there. Before I knew what was happening we were high above the village. When we came down in Ebem it was a strangely Americanized place with wide paved sidewalks and shops fronted by large plate-glass windows without the iron bars that typically cover windows in Nigeria. Behind the glass were displays of toys and chic home furnishings. Suddenly, and incongruously, some Nigerian government soldiers spotted us and began to chase us. My friend showed me how to avoid them by becoming invisible. This was done by moving through the spaces where the pursuers were not focusing their attention. Finally we eluded them, and it became so dark I could no longer see my companion but only hear the sound of his footsteps. Then he turned and embraced me. He said he was very pleased with me and that it was time for me to be initiated.

I woke abruptly feeling uneasy and haunted. Then in a rush of rationalization I began to analyze the dream. The meaning seemed clear enough: flying to an Americanized Ebem anticipated my return

to the States. The dream reflected Ink's—and perhaps my own—
concern that I should be initiated before I returned. The whole issue
of initiation had been lurking in the back of my mind for some time
and my trip to Aba to buy dibịa supplies brought it into dream
consciousness: a reassuringly rational explanation. Yet I could not
help but feel that perhaps I should take this call to service seriously.
Dreams are a common medium for communications from entities
like Agwu as well as from ancestral spirits. Could I afford to ignore
such an unambiguous directive to undergo initiation? These questions were overshadowed by the simple fact that, as an anthropologist, I could not resist telling Ink about my dream if only to see what
would happen.

Ink had traveled to northern Nigeria for a teachers' conference,
and I didn't see him for a week. In the interim I mentioned the
dream to no one. In Ink's absence I spent time in Akanu with other
friends tying up loose ends of my research and taking part in local
events. I spent some days with my friend Joe Agara, and we took
leisurely strolls around Akanu as I asked him questions on various
topics. On one of these strolls, as we were passing the largest meetinghouse in the village, a man ran up and told us that Nna Kalu
Omiko wanted to see us. I knew Kalu Omiko by reputation but had
never formally met him. He was a powerful chief in the village as
well as an elder of the Ekpe secret society and a highly renowned
dibịa. Ink had told me most of the villagers were afraid of him, and it
was easy to see why. His appearance was singularly striking. He had a
long, full white beard and a blind right eye that was completely
white. Aside from his startling appearance, his intensity was overpowering. When he fixed you in the piercing gaze of his left eye you
could not help but to freeze in your tracks. He had a force of personal
presence that marked him as one of the most powerful dibịa in the
region. We went to his home, located just beyond the meetinghouse. It consisted of two small rooms, the first of which was
crowded with patients, some plastered with muddy looking poul-
tices. The floor and shelves were stacked with large bundles of various roots and herbs. I sent for a bottle of gin with which Kalu Omiko
offered a brief libation. He was a bit drunk and addressed me with
great intensity. Though his apprentice encouraged him to speak in

Ohafia dialect, the old man spoke to me slowly and with evident effort in broken English. He recalled to me that he had been there when I danced through the village at the culmination of my initiation into the Ekpe secret society. Then he lurched forward and whispered: "And now you will be initiated as a dibịa!" A cold chill ran through me. Did this man know my dreams?

## Eye-Opening Experiences

I was beginning to realize just how much anxiety I felt regarding the possibility of an initiation ceremony. The initiation of a dibịa is said to "open the initiate's eyes," meaning that the process enables the dibịa to see things noninitiates cannot see. I witnessed such a rite during my first stint of fieldwork in 1989. The initiate was a young boy whose father was bearing the enormous expense of the sacrifices, feasts, and other offerings and gifts. The ceremony went on for four days, the first three of which were conducted in secret. I knew little of what happened during this period of seclusion but I had heard that it involved, among other things, the application of hot pepper juice and certain psychoactive herbs to the eyes. This was done by forming spherical bundles of the herbal materials and soaking these in palm wine. The bundles were then squeezed so as to apply the infusion to the initiate's eyes. For this reason the ceremony was referred to as *Itu Ọgwụ* (to squeeze medicine).

On the final day the boy was brought into the interior yard of his compound, which was packed with observers. Three drummers played in chorus on tortoise shells struck with antelope horns. The boy was secluded in a small, makeshift initiation tent constructed of cloth wrappers. A dog was carried into the crowded yard by two men. The creature was full of fear, sensing that he was going to be killed. A high tension filled the crowd as several men finally managed to restrain the snarling, snapping animal. As the dog's throat was cut a visible relief spread through the crowd. The man wielding the knife quickly removed the dog's eyes and took them into the tent where the boy was sequestered. The tortoise drumming accelerated and

Fig. 2.   "It is to be understood that the boy's eyes have been
replaced with those of the dog. Now he will be able to see
spirits just as dogs are able to see spirits." *(Akanu Ohafia 1990)*

after a long interval the boy was finally carried out of the tent apparently unconscious. One of the men carrying him was holding leaves
over the boy's eyes, and blood was pouring off of his face from under
the leaves. In hushed tones, Ink whispered to me, "It is to be understood that the boy's eyes have been replaced with those of the dog.
Now he will be able to see spirits just as dogs are able to see spirits."[1]
The boy was carried away, and the music continued. The mood of the
crowd became festive, and palm wine flowed freely. The air was filled
with the familiar sounds of an Ohafia festival: music and voices
raised in laughter and good-natured squabbling.

      After quite some time the festivities were disrupted by the ini-
tiate who ran into the yard and then stopped abruptly, cringing and
looking around wildly like a frightened animal. The eyes bulged
from their bloody sockets like those of a madman. For a moment
everything stood still, but then the initiators who were pursuing
him entered the yard, and the chase continued. He was quickly

cornered and subdued. The initiators surrounded him, holding him firmly and giving him palm wine infused with herbs. After a short time he became calm, and they moved away leaving him sitting unhindered in front of the initiation tent. A small bundle of leaves was set at his feet. He picked it up and examined it closely, then placed it back on the ground and closed his eyes. After a moment he announced the bundle consisted of four beans wrapped in four leaves. His mother came forward, opened the bundle, and displayed the contents, declaring the accuracy of her son's prediction. Cheers rose up. It was over. The initiate had successfully "seen the unseen" (*igba aja*).[2] The acquisition of this extraordinary vision marked the initiatory passage. This ability to see what the uninitiated could not see distinguished the dibịa from the layman.

## A Compromise

At the end of the week Ink arrived at my home with the completed dibịa hat in hand. Before I could say anything he looked at me gravely and told me he had something very important to tell me. He sat, paused, and then smiled. He told me that on the night following our trip to the market he'd had a dream. His late father had come to him and asked about me and the need to initiate me. Ink had expressed concern to his father regarding the expense and the "inconveniences" of initiation. In reply, Ink's father had reminded him that there were two types of dibịa initiation. There was the full-fledged and very expensive *Itu Ọgwụ* initiation and the lesser *Itu Anya Olu* ceremony (to squeeze one eye only). The latter rite could be performed without much public involvement. All that was required was participation by the initiate's "master" (in my case Ink), a few representatives of the paternal compound, and some senior members of the village's "Night Society" (Atulị Abalị, the secret society that oversees all dibịa activities). Ink showed little surprise when I told him of my own dream. He was confident that the man I described was his father. My dream was only a confirmation of something already obvious to him: that I needed to be initiated before I returned home because, if troubles with Agwu began in the States, there would be few means of recourse. He said he would keep the dibịa hat for eight days in the large box that housed the dibịa tools in his Agwu shrine. Then we would ritually consecrate it and the initiation could be done two days later.


## A Death in the Family

In the meantime there were preparations to be made. An order for a large quantity of palm wine needed to be arranged. The necessary herbs would have to be gathered by other dibịa assisting in the ritual. Sacrificial items had to be acquired; several bottles of whiskey and gin, natural chalk, two cocks, and various ritual necessities including kola pepper (*oso oji*) and red and yellow pigment powders (*ufie* and *odo*).[3] Most important were the cloth wrappers that Ink and I would wear during the ceremony. They needed to be made from red, black, and white cloth sewn together in strips. Ink explained that black and white indicated the positive and negative aspects of the power one acquired through Agwu: the ability to heal and the ability to harm. Red signified the danger involved in mediating these forces and the skill necessary to integrate them properly. In time, we found appropriate fabrics in the local markets and took them to a tailor for assembly. When the wrap-cloths were finished Ink and I traveled together to Ink's natal compound in Akanu where the ceremony would take place.

When we arrived we found a member of Ink's age-set waiting for him. A meeting was being held, and members were being pressured to pay up the remainder of their contributions toward the group's community project. Ink's age-set had spent the last few years bringing electricity to the village. It had been an expensive endeavor involving the purchase of transformers and cable as well as a tremendous amount of labor. Ink went on to the meeting but I stayed behind. Basking in the cool of the evening I settled into an armchair in the yard and read a novel by lamplight. Soon three boys arrived looking for Ink. In whispered tones they informed Ink's senior wife, Chinyere, that Ink's mother's brother, Nna Nduka, had just died. By the time Ink returned he had already learned of this. He sat down with me and said with great solemnness, "something has happened!" He repeated this several times to emphasize the significance of the event.

Nna Nduka had been a very old man, and he died after a long period of illness. When I met him he had been friendly and even jovial, but he required medication to make bearable his constant pain. The tremendous significance of Nna Nduka's death centered on his standing in the community. He had been the oldest man, and head, of his maternal descent group. He had been an Ekpe member and an acclaimed hunter. In short, he had been, as the Ohafia put it, a hero.

Since rights to agricultural property are held by the maternal descent groups, the death of a chief initiates a process of succession. The burial of a chief is a time when both paternal and maternal relatives of the deceased reposition themselves as ranking members of descent groups. A chief's burial must reflect his greatness, and a grand funeral is a real test of the financial and social resourcefulness of relatives. Those who are able and willing to invest in giving their "father" a grand burial will be able to invoke the memory of their contributions during negotiations for land access and other privileges. Ink always excelled at positioning himself well at such moments. Nna Nduka was his mother's brother; hence the role he played in the burial would prove instrumental in descent group affairs for some time to come. In addition, Nna Nduka's senior son, though relatively wealthy, had repeatedly exhibited a lack of enthusiasm for traditional displays of largesse. In fact, Nna Nduka had confided to Ink that he feared his son might not "know how to bury him properly," and he had asked Ink to make sure he was not disgraced in his final rites.

The death was a good one. This man had lived a long and honorable life. No one could ask for more than that. It was time for the great celebration. The moral obligation placed upon Ink to see that his mother's brother was properly buried offered a unique opportunity to position himself in relation to other members of his matrilineage in a way that would lead to clout, power, and wealth. Unfortunately, Ink had just been taxed by his age-grade for all the cash he had on hand. (Ink suggested that they had known of Nna

Nduka's death and had rushed to claim his debt before he found out himself.) Even though it was nearly midnight, a wake was beginning, and people were waiting to see who would supply the drinks. While Ink refused all attempts to pay him for his extensive assistance in my research I knew that this refusal created the obligation of brotherly generosity in such times of need. I saw my opening and gave Ink a stack of bills, enough to keep people in gin throughout the night.

I woke the next morning to the predawn sound of the hunter's horn played in honor of Nna Nduka who had been one of the hunters guild's senior members. Ink had gone out, but returned shortly explaining that he had bought a goat on credit for the burial feast later that day. Unflappable, Ink insisted we should proceed with my initiation in spite of the unforeseen developments. One of Ink's children arrived with the cock we had ordered, and we began the dedication of the hat and the dibịa cloth at once. I switched from trousers to a simple wrap cloth so as to be suitably formal for the occasion. Ink called his eldest son Nduka to join us as we entered the Agwu shrine established by Ink's father. His four-year-old son Ibem ran to join us also. Ink quipped that Ibem planned to be a dibịa himself so he never missed a chance to observe his father at work. At one end of the room was Agwu's "face" (*ifu* Agwu),[4] the central feature of which was the large wooden box that served both to store tools and as an altar. Ink removed the hat from the interior and placed it, with the dibịa cloth, on the box. Ink's elder son Nduka brought the cock, a bottle of gin, and a knife. Ink took the gin and offered libations. First he poured wine at the entrance to the hut, calling ancestors to join in the ceremony. Then he poured wine before the "face" for Agwu and for his father. He took a large piece of chalk and, scraping it with his nails, made a large mound of white powder in the palms of my outstretched hands as he pronounced a blessing upon me and my future as a dibịa. He rubbed chalk on my forehead and instructed me to rub my hands over my face covering it with white dust. Then he sprinkled chalk and red and yellow pigment on the hat and the cloth, blessing them and consecrating them to dibịa work. He called to Nduka to bring the cock and the knife. Squeamish, Nduka handed the cock to Ink and then turned away, going to the window and keeping his head outside through the whole procedure. Little Ibem, however, watched with great concentration everything that took place. Ink scraped the feathers from the fowl's neck and cut its throat. He dripped blood over the stones at the front of the face. He dripped blood over the chalk, the red and yellow pigments, and the kola pepper. He broke the pepper open, and we each ate seven of the hot seeds. Then we both took a shot of gin, and the dedication was done. Nduka exited quickly but Ibem stood firm and announced that he wanted to lie by my side on the day of the ritual and be initiated with me. Ink laughed and told me that this bold four-year-old, who had danced with the men at my Ekpe initiation while other children watched in awe, had told him to initiate him into dibịa as soon as possible because Ink needed a professional heir and his older brother showed no interest. We both laughed and praised Ibem for his bravery and his devotion to his father's craft.

## A Passage

Ink and I walked down the rutted path from his hilltop compound into the old village center. Our first stop was the compound of the man who was the successor to Nna Nduka as chief of the maternal descent group. His small sitting room was crowded with men. A young man was holding a bottle of gin and a shot glass and slowly moving from man to man, filling the glass and giving each his share. Discussions were going on, and the room reverberated with shouting. The scene was quite familiar. Before I understood Ohafia styles of discourse I would have called this arguing, but the ritualized drinking and the heightened stridency of speech simply marked this as a discussion of matters of importance. They were talking over plans for the day's proceedings. Ink's primary interest was to see how the gin supply was holding out. Finding them well stocked, we stayed for a while but passed up the opportunity to drink. Ink advised me that studied restraint would have to be exercised today if we were to avoid becoming completely "soaked." He intended to drink only when he arrived at the house of the deceased.

Nna Nduka's compound was in a newer section of Akanu named *Faith* by the missionaries who established it. The cool of the morning was giving way to the heat of midday by the time we trekked past the small contiguous huts of the old village toward the outlying settlements of new homes, many with second stories and spacious inner courtyards. We found Nna Nduka's compound crowded with people dressed in fine clothing: men in heavy velvet shirts and madras wrappers, women wrapped in bright imported cloth from India and Holland. As we entered the yard we were quickly ushered in to view the deceased. Nna Nduka's body was displayed in a coffin in a small room packed with women. When I looked at this skeletal cadaver with cotton in its nose I could not recognize the man whom I had seen, alive and jovial, just a few weeks before. I found it difficult to concentrate on responding correctly to the profusion of greetings because, even though I had attended many of these events, I had never learned to be casual in the presence of a corpse.

We moved into a large room filled with men and women chatting and drinking. No beer or palm wine seemed to be forthcoming and I was resolved to avoid gin, so I deflected the shot glass as it was passed, touching it to acknowledge the hosts' generosity but sending it on its way. Nna Nduka's eldest son, the primary sponsor of the event, sat sipping gin, and Ink kept directing barbed remarks at him. At first I wondered if this indicated some sort of traditional "joking relationship" but I discovered later that Ink was furious with his wealthy relative for the paucity of the preparations. If this first burial ceremony was to be such a meager event, then what, worried Ink, would the second burial be like? The second burial was customarily held many months, sometimes years, following the death of an important individual. The delay allowed family members time to raise funds for an event splendorous enough to be an appropriate tribute to the deceased. Ink asked when the second burial would be held. The elder son responded that he would hold it in August. Ink insisted that no one would be around in August during "ụnwụ"—the time of scarcity before harvest when much of the population migrates to urban residences. Ink proposed the ceremony should be planned for December when everyone returns for Christmas festivities. "I often travel in December because I am frequently invited to visit good friends in distant places at that time," came the curt reply. Ink coolly countered: "Then you must invite those good friends to Ohafia to attend the burial of your own father!" This retort was met with silence, and Ink continued with the provocation, "or perhaps you should hold the ceremony after *izu atụ* [eight days]."[5] This provocation was ironic; it would be impossible to produce an adequate second burial ceremony in such a short time. The switch from reference to the Roman calendar to Ohafia time reckoning was significant. Izu atụ has significance as an indigenous measurement of ceremonial time. To speak of it in this context, when the man's adherence to traditional obligations was in question, was to twist a rhetorical knife. Unable to counter Ink's offensive he mumbled something about the possibility of a December ceremony and then quickly tried to change the subject.

This awkward sociality was abruptly brought to a close by the sound of a drum calling mourners to the graveside. Nna Nduka was to be buried traditionally, and a grave, eight feet in depth, had been dug into the floor of his sitting room—the central room of this large compound. All the furniture had been removed, and dirt was piled up against the walls blocking the two internal doors. The drum was announcing that Nna Nduka was to be put into the earth. The drummer played the small three-footed drum (*esin*) with two sticks, articulating the drum's voice with the butt of his hand. In this way he produced the tonalities necessary to speak with the drum, calling mourners and singing the praises of the late man. As the drummer played he shouted a high piercing tone in the manner characteristic of Ohafia war dance drummers. Two young men, dressed only in wrap-cloths tied short in the warrior fashion, jumped into the grave pit, and the coffin was carried into the room. It remained open as the men lowered it into the grave. More men in warrior garb entered from the central court of the compound, dancing and shouting. When the coffin was secure in the grave one of the men in the pit straightened the head and limbs of the cadaver. This was done because it is said that people who are carelessly buried with their body out of alignment will suffer from a parallel deformity in their next incarnation. When this final task was completed the coffin lid was lowered into place and nailed. Ink and Nna Nduka's eldest son (representing the maternal and paternal lineages) came to the graveside, and each tossed handfuls of dirt into the grave. Both dabbed tears from their eyes with handkerchiefs. The music accelerated and the drummer began to sing more ardently. The dancers commenced shouting and danced with great leaps around the grave.

The room was crowded with people, more so because most of the floor space was displaced by mounds of dirt. I found myself having to actively resist the pressure of bodies packed in behind me to avoid inching toward the gaping pit that spread like a great open mouth only a few inches in front of me. In a moment of vertigo, my discussion with Ink regarding traditional burial practices came rushing to memory. He had told me that in previous times men were buried with the heads they had taken in battle. But a great chief could not be buried with just a few skulls. Someone, a slave or a stranger, had to be thrown alive into the grave, buried alive with the honored dead to demonstrate that he was a great man. I had spent months trying to get a feel for the logic of human sacrifice for, though it hadn't been practiced in a century, I felt Ohafia people understood its meaning in a way that totally eluded me. My imminent initiation loomed in my mind. This tomb in the earth evoked the dark abyss of unfathomable cultural knowledge into which I was about to plunge, or perhaps be pushed, by forces that, though I didn't comprehend them, were becoming increasingly tangible in my life.

I stumbled dizzily from the house into the hot afternoon air. Ink grabbed my arm and suggested we return to the old village after one last drink. As we strolled down the broad red dirt road some men ran up to Ink asking him to donate money for gunpowder so a salute to the late man could be fired. He dismissed them angrily, growling "It's the son's responsibility!" Then Ink began to rail about the poor execution of the ceremony. Nna Nduka had feared it would be so because his son's failure to participate in his age-grade, in descent group affairs, and in the community in general indicated selfishness and a disregard for traditional custom and values. He should have provided gunpowder to announce the burial, and a great volley should have sounded as the coffin went into the earth. There should have been beer and palm wine and meat available rather than only gin. There should have been music, and he didn't even hire an ambulance to bring the body from the hospital, only a bush taxi. (At this comment Ink imitated the sound of the poorly running taxi—"putt-putt-putt-putt.") Ink complained that Nna Nduka's body had been "poorly dressed," but the thing that irked him most was that, in wanton disregard of traditional signs of respect appropriate to the occasion, the son had worn trousers to the graveside rather than a wrap-cloth. We returned to the compound of the chief of Ink's matrilineage. Most of the other maternal kin had also been to the burial and were exhibiting various degrees of drunkenness. The discussions continued as before, in argumentative tones. As the exchange progressed I noticed a December date for the second burial now seemed to be taken for granted.

## The Women "Riot"

The next day various dibịa met to discuss arrangements for my initiation ceremony. The first to arrive was Kalu Ibe with whom I had studied divination techniques. Then others arrived including a man named Awa from Ink's paternal family. Ink had informed me that Awa's skill playing the tortoise shell drum (*ekwe mbe*) would contribute to the proper execution of the ceremony. We discussed the ceremony and the herbs each of them were to gather from the bush. Many of the plants were types with which I was not familiar, and they were referred to euphemistically, increasing my curiosity. At one point Ink insisted that something Awa suggested was inappropriate. I was comforted when I realized Ink was negotiating for a minimal level of hot pepper juice in the infusion that would go into my eyes. Awa then became belligerent, arguing that I should provide a dog. Ink countered that a dog was not necessary: the ceremony would not include an "eye transplant," and the small number of participants would only require a cock to feed them. Finally, Awa reluctantly conceded. The meeting concluded with general consensus but Awa's contentiousness concerned me. I had learned from experience that individuals who put forth contrary arguments during the planning stages of a ceremony may also employ other techniques of subversion. As the meeting ended we found we needed one more tortoise shell drum for the ceremony, and I decided to go back to Amaekpu to get my own. Ink was planning to attend a wake for a maternal kinsman that night, and I didn't return to Akanu until the next morning. When I arrived I found Ink sitting in the shade of his yard. Smiling, he invited me to join him so that he could tell me of an intrigue that had unfolded in my absence.

After I had left the previous day, Ink had returned to the site of the burial where a new floor was being installed over the grave. Once a smooth finish to the floor was attained a closing ritual was enacted. Nna Nduka's senior wife brought the clay soup bowl and the gourd yam dish she had used for serving her husband. She shattered these on the new floor, thus signifying the end of her service to her late husband and her freedom to remarry. Subsequent events continued through the evening, and while Ink was occupied with his maternal kin a plot to thwart my pending initiation was being hatched among some of his paternal relations.

When I had originally arrived in Ohafia, I had come with the blessings of a school colleague who was a member of Ink's paternal family. As I grew to know the people of the family it became clear that Ink was someone who fully understood my mission in Ohafia and who would be of great assistance. However, some members of his family felt Ink's involvement with me was a monopolization of the status and wealth they associated with the researcher whom their brother in America had "sent to them." Ironically, it was those family members who had shown the least interest in my project who were the most resentful of Ink's easy commerce with me.

Perhaps as a result of this long-smoldering resentment, the news of my initiation had reached the women of Ink's paternal family in a somewhat distorted form. As the story spread among them it was said that Ink had already initiated me and that he had revealed the secrets of dibịa to me without consulting anyone. The blood in the Agwu shrine remaining from the consecration of the hat was said to be evidence of a completed initiation. Word of this spread rapidly, and within a short time the women were (to use Ink's term) "rioting," proclaiming that Ink had desecrated his father's Agwu shrine and demanding that the men of the compound do something about it.

Awa called a meeting of the Night Society in the traditional fashion, by playing a distinctive pattern on a double bell. But rather than using the standard small instrument he used a large one, signifying that a serious offense had occurred. Awa told the assembly that Ink had conducted a private initiation and had revealed all the secrets to me. He cited the protesting women as evidence that action must be taken. It was no accident that this meeting was called while Ink was at the other end of the village attending the funeral of his mother's late brother and was therefore unable to defend himself. Fortunately, Kalu Ibe, my divination instructor, was present at the gathering and spoke in my—and Ink's—defense. He recalled to them that Ink had brought me before the Night Society two years before and that they had all given their blessings to my studies.

I remembered that meeting well. I had only been in Akanu three days and was greatly heartened at my warm reception by this group of dibịa. At that time I did not specifically intend to study traditional medicine, but they nevertheless assured me that they would teach me everything. Only one outward gesture signified the distance between us, so great in regard to cultural knowledge. Ink instructed me that when chalk was passed I should rub it on the back of my wrist and not, under any circumstances, imitate the dibịa who would rub it next to their left eye. When people gather, the sharing of chalk signifies a peaceful affinity. But the "white eye" of the dibịa signifies that the bearer has been initiated and can "see" as dibịa can see.

After reminding the gathered men of the original agreement to work with me, Kalu Ibe assured the assembly that the initiation had not yet taken place and was not to be conducted in secret. He revealed that the way Awa knew of the event was because he had been asked to assist, as had Kalu Ibe himself. He confirmed that Ink had asked others to join the ceremony as well. Kalu Ibe began questioning Awa, asking why he hadn't mentioned the meeting with Ink or the fact that Kalu Ibe had also been there. Kalu Ibe also told the Night Society the story of my dream and that of Ink's. The fact that the impetus for the initiation had come through the intervention of Ink's father, who had been a powerful and highly renowned dibịa, was seen as a very compelling argument for the propriety of Ink's intentions. In this way, Kalu Ibe succeeded in forestalling any action on the part of the Night Society. In fact, after Kalu Ibe's testimony the focus of the meeting turned to Awa's liability and whether he should be considered guilty of malicious slander of a fellow dibịa.

Ink told me he suspected his brother, Kalu Nwosu, was scheming behind the scenes. He had invited this brother to join the initiation but Kalu Nwosu had been elusive since then. Ink knew the man bore a grudge about Ink's involvement with me. (This had become evident long ago when Ink had intervened in Kalu Nwosu's attempt to charge me a fee to participate in the compound's New Yam celebrations.) Ink had invited Kalu Nwosu to join in the hat dedication, but he had been "unavailable." Even so, Ink had sent him his rightful share (as Ink's senior brother) of the meat from the sacrificed cock. In fact, Ink had anticipated a certain degree of resistance to the initiation from resentful kinspeople, and throughout the planning he had paid scrupulous attention to traditional protocol.

Having updated me on these new developments, Ink and I walked into the old village to get palm wine for the rite. On our way we stopped to talk with the chief of the Night Society, who was sitting in front of the village meetinghouse with other elders. He greeted us and bade us join him in his own room. He led us through the narrow maze of corridors leading from the mouth of the compound and finally arrived at a small cubicle that turned out to be his Agwu shrine. The chief expressed support for my initiation and asserted that Awa should be fined a dog for his offense. Nevertheless, because of the conflict he wanted to perform divination to determine whether my initiation would be auspicious at that time. He produced an anthropomorphic bundle of plant material with long limbs of single straws. This he handed to Ink, and then he drew some lines on the floor with chalk. Ink held the object by the straws, and it skipped across the floor and then stopped. Ink looked at the chief who nodded, took the device from him, and handed it to me. I held it on the floor and examined the chalk marks. The object stood idle as I puzzled over the pattern of chalk. Ink coached me: "don't try to think, let it go on its own." I put a little downward pressure on the straws and the thing began to hop about. It wandered a bit and then stopped at the foot of the face where the chief's ancestral dibịa tools were displayed. Again the chief nodded, and he took the straw object from me. He said the initiation would be a success and that he would join us in the ceremony.

After our meeting with the chief we collected the palm wine, stopping by Kalu Ibe's to let him know the ceremony was about to begin. We then went to pick up some additional bottles of gin and whiskey. By the time we arrived back at Ink's compound Kalu Ibe, the dibịa chief, and another elder from the Night Society had already arrived. Ink had sent a child to remind Awa to attend, and he became concerned that he was not yet present. Although I had become wary of Awa, Ink insisted Awa's participation was essential precisely *because* he had publicly challenged the ceremony. Awa's involvement would deflect any objections that the ceremony had proceeded unlawfully. We went back into the village, ostensibly to get more kola, but also to find Awa. He was not to be found nor was the elusive Kalu Nwosu. Ink left a message to remind Kalu Nwosu to join the ceremony, and we proceeded up the main road toward the kola vendor. As we were sitting in the shade in front of a market stall Ink drew my attention to a figure across the village, barely discernible through the waves of heat convection. He was entering the compound we had just left. "It is Kalu Nwosu looking for Awa," Ink laughed. "He will find no Awa, only our invitation." When we returned to Ink's compound Awa was there, and Ink greeted him warmly. I reassured myself that Ink knew what he was doing. As I greeted Awa I felt confident the herbs he brought would do me no harm. In a final act of ruthless etiquette, Ink sent his son Nduka to find Kalu Nwosu and invite him to join us. Ink instructed me to dress for the ceremony: I was to wear nothing but the dibịa cloth. The assembled dibịa went into the compound and begin preparations for the rite. I sat in the shade of the yard wrapped in the red, white, and black cloth and pondered what the next few hours might bring.

## I Become a Dibịa

As I sat waiting, a good friend of mine named Mr. Uka arrived unexpectedly. He was accompanied by two women who were apparently teachers like himself. They had come on a condolence visit on Ink's behalf due to the death in his family. Mr. Uka was dressed in a neatly tailored English business suit, and the women were also in "church" finery. I had never met the women, but I knew Mr. Uka well. Although he was fully aware of my interest in Ohafia culture he was clearly puzzled to see me barefoot and bare-chested dressed in a dibịa cloth. Ink emerged from the compound, greeted them warmly, offered them drinks, and told them he was engaged in my initiation at the moment and that they would have to bear with us until it was completed. Mr. Uka grimaced and shook his head in disbelief. As we sat together he expressed his confusion. Though he knew of my scholarly interest in Ohafia culture, this initiation made no sense to him. I joked with Uka trying to draw the parallel between himself, an Ohafia man dressed in a European business suit, and myself, an American dressed as a dibịa. The irony was not at all apparent to him. In his own view, his movement toward a European life-style, occupation, and dress seemed logical, even natural. But my movement toward such a serious embrace of Ohafia traditions was incommensurable with every notion he had regarding the relationship between our two societies. I was still far from resolving Uka's confusion when I was called in to begin the ceremony.

I was led into a dimly lit alcove and told to sit on the grass mat which was on the floor. The dibịa chief began playing a tortoise shell and all the men began to sing as they crowded into the tiny room. Brief call and response songs followed one after the other. In the chorus I thought I heard a child's voice blending with the rest. I turned my head and saw that little Ibem had joined the others. As song filled the air, Kalu Ibe rubbed red and yellow pigment all over my body. A large clay bowl (*ọja*) was on the floor next to me filled with palm wine, and a ball of bundled leaves the size of a grapefruit lay submerged in its center. The air was heavy with the odor of wine and herbs. When Kalu Ibe had thoroughly covered me with the red and yellow pigments he picked up the dripping ball and began throwing the herb-infused palm wine at me in sharp bursts. He methodically soaked me with palm wine from every angle, and then, telling me to lie down, he drenched me again beginning at my feet and working his way up to my head. They laid palm fronds on me and continued singing for quite some time. I lay there, soaking wet, not having a clue as to what was going on. I tried to follow the words of the songs, grasping at references to tortoise, the obscure allegory, and meaningless syllabics. I strained for some clue to the structure, some essential core of meaning. Slowly the futility of analysis led me to still my thoughts. My researcher persona fell away, and I came into a full awareness of myself as a man undergoing an initiatory ordeal. I realized that I must yield to the process and that my main task was to do so stoically and willfully like an Ohafia warrior. A state of calm emptiness overcame me.

At length, Kalu Ibe took the fronds off and pulled me up abruptly. He placed a single palm leaf in each hand, and they led me out of the small room. As we moved toward the Agwu shrine we passed through the yard where Uka and the two women sat chatting. I was dripping with palm wine, streaked with red and yellow powders, and covered with wet herbs. The women averted their eyes, and Uka looked on with a pained expression that was not relieved by the smile and nod I gave him as I passed.

When we entered the Agwu shrine I was led to Agwu's face. Ink brought forth another bottle of gin and poured libations calling his father and other ancestral dibịa of the family to join in the proceedings. Then a long series of orations by Ink, Awa, Kalu Ibe, and finally the dibịa chief served to introduce me to Agwu. The singing and tortoise shell drumming began again, and Kalu Ibe took the palm leaf from my left hand and whipped my shoulder with it twice, producing a cutting pain. He whipped my left hand and left foot several times and then moved behind me and whipped the left shoulder, hand, and foot again. Then he folded the leaf into a small club and thwacked me hard on the head. He placed the leaf on the face and repeated the whole procedure with the palm leaf in my right hand, this time whipping the right side of my body. Momentarily the singing ceased, and Awa approached me with the large chunk of chalk I had provided. He shaved powder from this into my outstretched palms, saying a blessing upon me as he did this. As I smeared the chalk on my face the singing began again. I looked at the faces of my comrades and realized these dibịa were genuinely pleased to have me among them. The spirit of celebration filled me, and I, for the first time, joined in the singing. After a long while we proceeded back to the other room, still singing. Soon I found myself back on the mat, bathing in palm wine once again. Kalu Ibe squeezed the rich infusion from the ball of herbs directly into my mouth. The others were now drinking from the pot also. Then other herbs were prepared. Kalu Ibe rolled them into a ball and soaked them. He squeezed a bit into his own mouth (a gesture demonstrating that it was not poison) and then wrung it repeatedly into my mouth soaking it in palm wine each time. A third bundle of plant material was prepared and soaked. He squeezed this directly into my eyes while insisting I should not blink. To my relief, the solution wasn't so harsh that I couldn't comply.

Finally Kalu Ibe called for the cock. He held it for some time, speaking the appropriate words of offering. Then he pulled me up and had me stand before him as he beat me with the live bird in the same manner as he had earlier with the palm leaves. The cock was large, and he wielded it with great force. It was everything I could do to keep my balance as he pounded on me. By the time he was finished the cock was unconscious. Kalu Ibe told me to lie down again, and he cut the bird's throat. Then he began dripping the blood over me very methodically working from toe to head. The remaining blood he poured directly into my mouth. By this point I was caught up in the rhythm of the ritual, and drinking blood seemed a reasonable thing to do. I imbibed the warm fluid and savored its rich flavor. The bird was plucked and the feathers were stuck all over my body, which was by now thickly coated with various sticky substances. We sat singing in the small room for quite a while and continued drinking palm wine from the constantly replenished bowl.

I wasn't sure it was over until Ink laughed and said "ụgbụa ị wụ onye dibịa" (you're a dibịa now). He placed the coveted dibịa hat on my head, and we walked back out into the yard where the schoolteachers sat having patiently waited for over two hours. Mr. Uka's distress was now, at last, mixed with humor as he saw me in my final, blood encrusted, quilled and feathered glory. Ink, wanting to preserve images of this historic moment for posterity, retrieved my camera from within the compound. He insisted we should photograph the visiting teachers first. I was the only person there who

Fig. 3.   Mr. Uka photographed me and the other dibịa in
various poses. *(Photo by O. Uka, Akanu Ohafia 1991)*

knew how to use the camera so the job fell upon me. I can only imagine how absurd it must have appeared as I, with a mouth dripping blood like a Hollywood ghoul, directed them into position to take advantage of the day's dwindling light. I admit I played the drama to the fullest, adjusting their positions with a professional concern for detail and quipping "I bet you never had such a well-dressed photographer." Even the women were laughing now.

## The White Eye of the Dibịa

I showed Mr. Uka how to use my camera, and he photographed me and the other dibịa in various poses. After the teachers left, Ink told his daughter to prepare a bath for me. Ironically, the long process of removing the tenacious layers of matter with a bucket of cold water and a plastic scouring pad proved to be more painful than anything I experienced in the ritual itself. By the time I returned to the yard, wrapped in a clean cloth, the cool dusk had settled on the hilltop compound. The bowl of herbal infusion had been brought out, and we continued to drink the rich liquid, talking and sporadically bursting into song. At first we discussed the ceremony. They praised my "toughness" in not flinching. This impression was due more to their assumption that Americans tend to be "soft" than to any real attempt to put me through an ordeal. The infusions had been fairly benign and had induced nothing more than a pleasant euphoria comparable to hashish. I was feeling remarkably exhilarated. Slowly, my attention slipped away from the conversation, and I became lost in contemplation of the vast star-studded sky above me. Suddenly, I was brought back to earth by sharp words addressed by the dibịa chief to Awa. He challenged him to explain his actions earlier in the day. Why should he not be charged a goat for the wrongful slander of a fellow dibịa? Awa was reticent for a few moments. Then he suddenly stood and began to sing. In his animated performance the whole story came out. The involvement of other players was revealed, and Awa's song bemoaned the fact he had been duped into risking his own reputation while others remained hidden.

When Awa's performance was concluded, a new argument ensued regarding how much he should be fined for his infraction. I lost interest and slipped back into my contemplation of the stars. I had now made my peace with Agwu. I no longer had to be concerned that the troublesome spirit would "bother" me upon my return to the United States. In addition, no charge of unauthorized involvement in dibịa affairs could again be raised against me. That issue had been permanently put to rest. But to what extent were these two negotiations the same thing? Durkheim would have argued that making peace with Agwu and making peace with the dibịa community formed a single process; that Agwu ultimately *was* the dibịa community and that the ceremony created the social fact of my membership by way of the social action of ritual.

But this argument seemed conspicuously superficial. The rite of passage marked a transformation of social ordering, a repositioning of myself in relation to the social whole. Certainly, the experience of that transformation had allowed me to "see" those social relations in relief. I had become aware of antagonisms and alliances that had previously been unexpressed or largely unknown to me. The process of bringing the ceremony into being had been as much of an illuminating experience as the ritual itself. But was there more to it than that? Though the wine, the herbs, the songs, the beating, and the ritual itself had left me feeling euphoric I couldn't say I felt any awakening abilities in the form of telepathic powers or occult vision. I certainly hadn't had any great mysteries revealed to me or received interpretations of esoteric signs as I had during my Ekpe secret society initiation. Yet I felt an exhilaration that seemed to blossom from a source more profound than mere intoxication.

As I leaned back, taking in the vastness of the night sky, I remembered the vividness of Ink's father in my dream and realized that I now felt comfortable in the assumption that it was in fact his father. I felt an overwhelming sense of liberation in the knowledge that I could—indeed that I must—allow the possibility of this ancestral influence in my own life. If I did not, then my participation would have been crassly hypocritical, a betrayal of my friends who so ardently argued my case on the grounds of Ink's father's intervention. I recalled Kalu Omiko's prescience of the initiation, and myriad other uncanny events I had experienced since my arrival in Ohafia that had been chipping away at the ontological foundations of my cultural preconceptions about reality. It was not that these phenomena inspired a "belief" in the certainty of some sort of "Ohafia worldview." Rather, my frame of mind was one of an enhanced uncertainty, and I realized that it was this uncertainty itself that was in some sense liberating. The knowledge of dibịa takes for granted that human experience is not reducible to known and predictable facts. And in this the traditional doctor displays a wisdom deeper than that of the positivist social scientist. The knowledge of dibịa resides not in formal "laws" but in a continual reading of the shifting and negotiable relations between things. I could not expect to gain these abstruse abilities instantly. After all, the ceremony hadn't transformed me into a dibịa, it had only given me the right to continue learning: to develop myself into a dibịa if I was able to master the skills and knowledge required. Still, a kind of new vision had in fact been realized in the course of my initiation. I had glimpsed another order of knowledge. My dream had forced the conceit of ethnographic observation to give way to the social necessity of participation. In response to my situation, these men had made a remarkable gesture of comradeship and I had become integrated into this community of healers and diviners. What significance did this fact have in my own life? Clearly the ramifications went beyond "social integration." I had gained access to the knowledge of the dibịa. It was now up to me to have the will and insight to engage and master this knowledge.

Soon Ink and I were walking the other men back to the old village center. By starlight we navigated the narrow rutted paths. Kalu Ibe showed me the secret dibịa handshake, and with that we parted. The next morning he showed up early at Ink's compound. As I drank my coffee he inquired after the herbal wine from the night before. There was still some left, and we gave him a cupful. At Ink's prompting, I tipped Kalu Ibe 200 naira. He had certainly earned it, not only for his leadership in the ritual but for his critical defense of Ink before the Night Society. Kalu Ibe put the money on the concrete floor of Ink's front porch. He offered libation to the ancestors, pouring the wine upon the floor next to the stack of bills. Then, using the same chunk of chalk that had provided blessing the day before, he scraped dust onto the bills and into the pool of wine. He mixed the chalk and wine into a paste with his finger and applied it, in the sign of the dibịa, to his left eye. Ink did the same and then, looking at me with a broad smile, said, "It is now your right too!" Mimicking my colleagues, I applied the chalk to my eye with an authoritative swipe, and we all took a cup of wine together.

## Reflections

The ethnographer straddles two worlds. Even those who study the cultures into which they were born must operate in terms of what Giddens (1986:374) calls a "double hermeneutic. . . . the intersection of two frames of meaning . . . the meaningful social world as constituted by lay actors and the metalanguages invented by social scientists." However, if the researcher assumed a priori ontological privilege for the latter frame, then ethnography becomes a sterile exercise in elegant theoretical modeling which shuns the complexity of the lived experience that these models putatively represent. Johannes Fabian (1983:165) concludes his important critique of anthropology with the assertion that we must "meet the Other on the same ground, in the same Time." The growing use of narrative accounts in ethnographic presentation and the muting of the omniscient explanatory voice of the theorist in works by Jackson (1982, 1989), Turner (1992), Fabian (1990), Stoller (1989b), Stoller and Olkes (1987), and others reflect an increased awareness of the necessity for placing indigenous modes of discourse and experience on an equal footing with scholarly methods. Far from being a question of mere style, this problem cuts to the theoretical core of anthropology. It demands much more than an intellectual repositioning of the researcher in relation to his or her data.

We must live the ethnographic experience *with* the people we study and reflect critically on our representation of that experience. If ethnography is not to be a recapitulation of colonial dominance then it must begin as cultural apprenticeship. As Stoller (1989a:156) has written, "Apprenticeship demands respect. . . . [A] deep respect for other worlds and other ideas, ideas often preposterous to our own way of thinking, is central to the ethnographic endeavor." The fact that Agwu is not a phenomenon that lends itself to the strictures of logical falsification may render it uninteresting to the Popperian philosopher. But Agwu's importance in Ohafia demands that the ethnographer give it open-minded consideration. For the knowledgeable dibia the question of whether Agwu is a "spirit" or a "social fact" is absurd. That Agwu must be contended with is more relevant than its categorization by inappropriate English terms. It is these processes of dealing with Agwu that provide the most reliable route to knowledge of Agwu, and the narrative method illustrates this process more vividly than any purely formulaic analysis could. As the initiate, I was stripped of my notebook, my tape recorder, my presumptions. Perhaps this is the reason I have difficulty reducing this particular episode to mere "data." Yet, this story provides a glimpse of my field experience that could not be captured in a more formalized presentation. The value of this account is not a function of what it explains but resides in the story in itself: an episode in one ethnographer's journey on the path from cultural observation to cultural participation.

# PART 2

# The Dance of Histories

"Truth": according to my way of thinking . . . doesn't necessarily mean the antithesis of error, but in the more fundamental cases only the posture of various errors in relation to one another.

(Nietzsche 1909:535)

Until lions have their own historians, tales of the hunt shall always glorify the hunter.

Igbo proverb

## CHAPTER 3

# The Flesh Melts

"*Kpaṅ-kpaṅ-kpa kpaṅ-kpaṅ-kpa kpaṅ-kpaṅ-kpa . . .*"[1] the sharp clicking of bamboo slats cuts through the din of the crowd gathered for the burial of an eminent chief. The hot midday air is heavy with red dust raised by hundreds of feet: dust mixed with the rich aroma of sweat and the fragrant vapor rising from large pots of palm wine. Several young, robust men in short, coarsely woven blue loincloths begin to move into the center of the large clearing in front of the village meetinghouse. Their muscular arms are draped with the long white hair of ram's manes, and on their heads are "leopard caps," each pierced with an eagle feather. They move with confidence and pride, but their leader seems even more imposing. Balanced on his head is a brightly painted board upon which human heads sculpted of wood are displayed. The heads also are flanked with ram's mane and wear leopard caps—*okpu agụ*. The commons is crowded with people of all ages, some talking, greeting, laughing, others maneuvering to find a good place from which to view the dancers. The dance leader, holding a small palm shoot in his mouth and a short flared cutlass in his right hand, stares fixedly ahead as he dances with short deliberate steps.

Three percussionists sit on a wooden bench defining one edge of the dance space. With casual concentration they tap out the heartbeat of the dance with bamboo slat instruments known as *akwataṅkwa*. A drummer begins to play an *ikperikpe ọgụ* (war drum).[2] It is not a dance rhythm, but drum language that is echoed by the *opu*, the antelope horn played by one of the dancers.[3] The voice of the drum calls:

Everyone should come forth!
Those in the bush come out!
Those on the road come out!
The day is charged!

An old man, dressed in a faded wrap-cloth of Indian madras, sits on a nearby stool and begins to shout: "Utugokoko kwe nụ!" and a response resounds from the crowd: "huh!" He shouts again, "Akanu kwenụ!! ... Ohafia kwe nụ!! ... Igbo kwe nụ!! ... Nigeria kwe nụ! ..." and each time the crowd responds with urgent approval.[4] Then the old man begins to sing the legend of Elibe Aja, the story of a brave hunter who kills a leopardess that is terrorizing the neighboring Aro people only to eventually meet his own end trying to stop a wild boar from destroying farms in Amuru. The music is fast, driving, insistent. The dancers in the circle are joined by other men, some mature, some mere boys. Each moves his feet in a rapid side-stepping pattern. They roll their shoulders in tight circles flexing their chests. Gradually, deliberately, the tempo builds. As the pace of the music increases the pectoral flexing accelerates. The men's chests pulsate with rippling undulations. This phenomenon is called *ọfụfụ*. As Joseph Agara put it, "when the music takes fire, the flesh melts."[5]

## Singing the Past

The men who sing *abụ agha,* "war songs," are Ohafia's official historians. Chukwuma Azuonye, a Nigerian linguist who has devoted years to the collection and analysis of the texts of Ohafia war songs, identifies them as Ohafia's most important genre of oral literature (1974:iii). Azuonye's study reveals that the song texts cover a broad range of themes. Among them are accounts of the origins of various traditions such as the use of eagle feathers to adorn warriors (136), the leopard as the symbol of Aro kingship[6] (398), the origin of palm wine (134), and the origin of the war dance itself (491). Other songs tell stories of great heroes of Ohafia: men and women who, by way of acts of extraordinary bravery and perseverance, embody Ohafia ideals of honor, achievement, and success.

Despite the obvious mythic and legendary dimensions of the texts, it is clear that many of these songs are stylized accounts of actual events. The story of the origins of Ohafia (Azuonye 1974:133) chronicles a migration from Isieke village in Ibeku a short distance to the west of the present-day Ohafia territory. Nsugbe (1974:16–17) contends that Ibeku traditional history concurs with the Ohafia account and that a commonality of particular Ikebu and Ohafia customs supports the verity of the migration story. In addition to accounts of the early wars, Kalu Igirigiri's composition *Ǫgụ Mmekọta Naijiria* (Azuonye 1990:75) recalls an Ohafia perspective on the Nigerian civil war, establishing that new songs continue to be composed to memorialize events of historic importance.

Focusing on the literary dimensions and historical content of the war dance, Azuonye's study is devoted exclusively to the texts. His explicitly stated goal is to demonstrate that Ohafia possesses an oral tradition comparable to the epics of classical Europe. His painstaking collection and translation of the corpus of war song texts accomplishes that goal. However, further appreciation of the value of this centerpiece of Ohafia culture requires going beyond establishing its merit in comparison to European traditions. The war dance is a complex event that includes music, instrumental speech, dance, costume, and the display of symbolic objects. An analysis that reduces these nonverbal elements to merely the context of performance privileges the verbal mode representation to an extent that the Ohafia people themselves do not. The Ohafia refer to this performance genre as *iri agha*. *Agha* means war. The term *iri* does not easily translate to English. As in many African languages, Igbo dialects do not use separate terms to distinguish categories of music and dance. *Iri* refers to music and dance simultaneously, and it also extends to comprehend drama and display.[7] The term *iri* implies an integrity of dance and music at the most fundamental level.

The war dance is designated by an interrelated complex of music, dance, the visual display of clothing, headdresses, and iconic markers. These elements constitute aural, bodily, and visual experiences that structure the participants' identification of themselves as Ohafia men and women: an identity grounded in their knowledge of their ancestral past. This process of identity structuring is, of course, socially complex. The young men who perform ọfụfụ experience the war dance in a different way than the elderly men who remember such endeavors but now concern themselves with evaluating renderings of the old stories. The unmarried women who dance a woman's dance at the periphery while admiring the exhibition of young male dancers have different interests than the married women who take pride in the celebration of the achievements of their husbands and sons. And at times, an exceptional woman finds in the legends of the warrior women of old a charter for life as a heroine. She may even earn the right to dance the war dance with the men.[8] Little girls watch with interest as small boys raise their own war dances, complete with headdresses displaying crudely carved heads. These boys rehearse as play the performance abilities that they will exhibit with skill as adults.

While some aspects of war drumming and dancing refer directly to the sung texts such as praise names in drum language and pantomimic enactments of the narrative, other elements, such as the chest rippling of ọfụfụ and the visual symbolism of gesture and costume, constitute nonverbal forms of expression that must be understood on their own terms. While not discounting the importance of the texts of the war songs, I want to emphasize that the somatic, musical, and visual aspects of performance are not subordinate to the texts but constitute parallel expressions and experiences that inform Ohafia notions of history and gender in direct and compelling ways.

### The Music Takes Fire

Ohafia people claim the musical instrument called *akwatankwa* originated in Ohafia. It is a homely device, two slats of bamboo struck together to produce concise rhythmic patterns. They must be held so that the hand forms a natural resonating chamber. Ensembles of three play in unison the aggressive timeline of the war dance.[9] These sticks, used to produce a single repeated rhythmic phrase, constitute the core of a complex performance that embodies the ancestral foundations of Ohafia notions of masculinity. A legacy of courage, aggressiveness, and achievement is infused in the sound of the akwatankwa

and the movements they induce through association. As the akwataṅkwa play, the war drum calls men to action: "Agwọ ntụ nọ
akarịka!" (There is a venomous snake in the grass!)[10] This is a call
to arms, a summons to dance, to be alert, and to arrive prepared for
action. The war drum and the antelope horn are battlefield instruments once used to communicate during raids. Many of the calls
these instruments produce during performance are traditional alarms
and commands, and they bring the tension and immediacy of actual
battle into the mood of the dance. When the drum and horn "talk,"
they are literally speaking: reproducing, in heightened and stylized
form, the tone contours and rhythmic patterns of language. These
phrases are drawn from the repertoire of announcements, greetings,
warnings, praises, and challenges that are common to the instrumental vocabulary. Some elements, such as personal names, vary, and
many names may share the same rhythm and contour, distinguishable only by consonantal variables too subtle to be articulated by the
instruments.[11] These elements are understandable by way of the context, both at a phrase level and by way of knowledge of the event
itself. Participants know who is being praised and who is being challenged, and this knowledge enables them to *hear* the name as it is
spoken by the drum or horn. The war drum also plays the dance
rhythm, fitting its tones tightly within the fast paced timeline. The
drummer sings a high-pitched note interjected sporadically throughout the performance that further increases the fervent tone of the
event. The ensemble is small; the sound "hot," and aggressive.

The rhythmic form of the war dance identifies a distinctly masculine genre of music. This point was emphasized to me during
music instruction I received from Joseph Agara from the Ohafia village Ndi Uduma Amoke. After teaching me to play the rhythm of the
war dance, he taught me to play a song from the women's *ure*
dance.[12] In contrasting the two he remarked:

> Naturally, the tempo of man's music, manly music, is not sup-
> posed to be the same tempo with female music. . . . Here in
> Ohafia, women have got their own tempo of music. . . . You can
> see the difference. [The war dance rhythm] is saying: [quickly]
> *taa-taa-ta-taa-taa-ta-taa-taa-ta-taa*, it's continuous movement,

very manly. [The women's ure dance] is saying: [much more slowly] *tan-tan, tan-tan-ta, tan-tan, tan-tan-ta, tan-tan, tan-tan-ta* . . . the tempo with which they play seems to cover the general female music tempo in Ohafia. We don't have women who play something outside that tempo. They may sing differently, but the tempo remains: *tan-tan, tan-tan-ta, tan-tan, tan-tan-ta.* (Agara 1991:17-A-00)[13]

"Manly" rhythm is typified by the fast, duple meter of the war dance. "Womanly" rhythm is typified by the slower, compound meter of the ure dance that resolves to 6/4 (hemiola). The timeline of the ure dance is segmented by regular pauses that divide the rhythm asymmetrically. The effect is a lilting movement of sound that is embodied in the swaying motion of women's dancing. In contrast, the war dance, as Mr. Agara put it, is "continuous movement, very manly." Never pausing, the war dance rhythm pushes ahead, creating a sense of moving forward. This is embodied in the ridged comportment and continuous fluid movement of the dancers, often compared to that of leopards. Men speak of the compelling quality of the war dance rhythm: that they cannot resist the call to dance, that the sound of akwatankwa push the dancers. Like a voice of the ancestors, the war dance induces men to do what they must do to be Ohafia men.

### The Flesh Melts

The sound of the war dance produces a direct link between the ancestral values that the music invokes and the bodily experience that it evokes. The undulating chest movement called ọfụfụ constitutes a *somatic* rather than a *semantic* association: an immediately experienced bodily cognizance rather than an abstract codified message. When the sound of akwatankwa drifts through the village many young men and boys respond physically to the call, executing the dance and performing ọfụfụ. The word *ọfụfụ* is unique to dialects in the Ohafia region. It is probably derived from the verb root *ifụ* (to blow, or to receive an electric shock.)[14] The common characteristic shared by electric shock, blowing, and ọfụfụ is the sense of a force moving through the body. In the case of ọfụfụ, this force is conceived of as the ancestral power of Ohafia warriors. Joseph Agara's interpretation is that the akwatankwa "push" this force, filling Ohafia men with the strength (*ike*) of their heroic ancestors that manifests as ọfụfụ. Ogbu Kalu, Ohafia indigene and professor of religious studies at the University of Nigeria-Nsukka, suggested that the undulating motion of the chest was a mimetic demonstration of the death spasms of a decapitated man—the victim of Ohafia warriors. When the sound of akwatankwa is heard, the insistent rhythm carries with it a sense of what it means to be an Ohafia man, a descendant of courageous warriors.

Ọfụfụ is a dramatic embodiment of this ancestral force and the masculinity associated with it. Its locus is the chest or *obi*. The term *obi* is used idiomatically in a manner similar to the way *heart* is in English. Thus, it is said of a happy person *obi ya dị ụtọ,* or "his obi is sweet." Idiomatic forms using *obi* are common. A hot obi (*obi ọkụ*) refers to a volatile temper, a big obi (*obi ukwu*) refers to generosity or to determination and willfulness. To contain or trap one's obi (*ijide obi*) means to keep one's temper. To say that a person's obi is white (*obi ya dị ọcha*) means that they are honest and forthright. Hence, various assignations referring to aspects of character and temperament are idiomatically attributed to obi. Of the courageous it is said that "obi dị ike," their obi is powerful. The performance of ọfụfụ transforms the *sense* of the powerful chest of a warrior into a dramatically embodied and experienced fact. Sound and movement form the fundamental aesthetic core of iri agha upon which layers of visual symbolism, instrumental praise, mimetic dance, and stories are layered. This relationship between the sound and movement of iri agha is deeply ingrained in Ohafia bodily praxis, so much so that compelling power of the dance is considered intrinsic. Chukwuma Azuonye (1974:344) while collecting traditional texts of Ohafia war dance singers recorded the following exchange between one of his research assistants and Mrs. Echeme Ogwo, wife of a master vocalist from Ebem:

*Mrs. Ogwo:* You will soon get to know the qualities that make it [iri agha] interesting. I say, to know the qualities that make it interesting. You will soon get to know it.

*Researcher:* But how can we get to know it if you will not tell us what it is?

*Mrs. Ogwo:* Ah! you mean I should specify it: the qualities that I find interesting in it? Ah! But from where did you people come? Have you ever heard it performed? Have you ever heard it performed anywhere?

*Researcher:* Yes.

*Mrs. Ogwo:* Did you find it interesting?

*Researcher:* But is it the same thing you find interesting in it that we find interesting?

*Mrs. Ogwo:* Yes, of course.

*Researcher:* I don't think so.

*Mrs. Ogwo:* It is!

*Researcher:* I don't think so.

*Mrs. Ogwo:* It is!

*Researcher:* I believe we find it interesting for different reasons.

*Mrs. Ogwo:* It all amounts to the same thing.


Mrs. Ogwo insisted that the appeal of iri agha was embodied in the performance itself. Hence it seemed to her that this meaning should be self-evident: so much so that she was unwilling to describe it in abstract terms. This is in keeping with Merleau-Ponty's cogent insights regarding the phenomenology of bodily communication. For example, Merleau-Ponty observes, "I do not see anger or a threatening attitude as a psychic fact hidden behind the gesture, I read anger in it. The gesture *does not make me think* of anger, it is anger itself" (1989:184, italics in original). Iri agha remains salient because it is closer to the bone than products or ideology. It combines the compelling power of music, the symbolic immediacy of visual art, and the somatic experience of dance to create aesthetically complex frames of experience.

Ethnological analysis requires a transformation of research experience into an ethnographic text. The ethnographer can easily misplace this reflexive mediation between experience and the interpretation of experience, imagining this interpretation to be integral to the events observed rather than a product of the researcher's analytical process. We may err in presuming that actions, sounds, and objects are *representations* or *signs*, which actors must *interpret* in reference to verbal categories. Music and dance in particular are known of and for themselves. The contents of gestures and postures of dance and the musical forms that evoke them require no verbal mediation, they impart without first being named. Yet these contents are clearly not innate in the actions themselves. If they were, bodily communication would be universally understandable.

> The sense of the gestures is not given, but understood, that is, recaptured by an act on the spectator's part. The whole difficulty is to conceive this act clearly without confusing it with a cognitive operation. The communication or comprehension of gestures comes about through the reciprocity of my intentions and the gestures of others, of my gestures and intentions discernible in the conduct of other people. (Merleau-Ponty 1989:185)

This "reciprocity of intentions and gesture" requires that members of a society participate in the production and reproduction of a corpus of bodily knowledge by way of their socially constituted activities.[15] Iri agha is an aesthetically framed typification of culturally specific dispositions and practices. It constitutes a collective experience that extends through time, linking the living to their predecessors through realized action. In this way, identification with a people extending through historical time is objectified through the immediacy of bodily activity. This notion is eloquently expressed by Ogba Kalu of Abia, Ohafia, who stated:

> Whenever [the war dance] is performed, our hearts brim with joy: because it is the umbilical cord with which we were born. Whenever we hear its rhythm, our hearts swell with joy: we think of the day of our birth and cherish the day of our death; we think of the day we shall raise our heads in pride and rejoice in anticipation of the day we shall grow rich. . . . So then, we are most happy to see it performed every time. (Azuonye 1974:96)

Like libation rituals, iri agha engages the performer with the past in a manner that collapses the temporal ontology that divides the living and the dead.[16] In this way, participants experience individual existence as a part of a greater whole. When they dance iri agha they position themselves in social time and space with their ancestors and *as* ancestors in the making. They come to know that to prevail in their own lives they must live like those who brought them into the world. The immediacy and accessibility of the past lies in the fact that the past subsumes the present by consuming it. Each moment "dies," but significant actions and events live on as traces—the artifacts and memories with which the past fills the present. In this warrior's dance the past is the final conqueror, ultimately incorporating all people and events into its fold.[17]

Various scholars have suggested that the relationship of Africans to their ancestors could only be understood in terms of a specifically African conception of time. This is the basis of Evans-Pritchard's theory of "structural time" (1940a:94) and Vansina's notion of "Great Time" (Vansina et al. 1964:372). The problem with these views, and the point at which I diverge from them, is the assumption that the distinguishing feature is a particular *conception* of time that is the product of a distinctively African mentality. I argue that we are concerned with a particular *experience* of time that derives from the social constitution of experience in particular African societies. Events such as the performance of iri agha are mechanisms that establish this socially constructed temporality. In doing so iri agha provides an experiential link between personal time and social time and thus between identity and history.

## Performing History

While iri agha is a means of representing important events and people of the past it is distinct from academic historiography. Iri agha brings values into action by way of a practical and immediately experienced logic of performance. Ohafia history, ethnicity, and indigenous notions of masculinity and power are thus evoked and vivified in relation to present-day experience. The war dance does not seek to contain or explain the past because it is more than a "representation": the sights, sounds, and bodily movements associated with iri agha are an experiential means of engaging the past and engaging with the ancestors. Through dancing, men link their sense of personhood, masculinity, and their somatic knowledge of themselves with a continuum of experience that extends beyond individuals to encompass a corpus of ancestral knowledge.

Despite the fact that epic genres such as iri agha are often identified by indigenes as "our method of history," ethnohistorians have traditionally been wary of performed genres. Henige's handbook on methods for field research in oral history warns against the idealizing character of performed histories and guides the researcher toward the more controlled and "objective" environment of interview: "While still in the field he can try to take measures to reduce the impact of the informants' *performing sense*—here is another advantage of the private interview" (Henige 1982:76, italics added).

However, epic texts are rich in detail and are often the original source of the historical "facts" revealed in interviews. They clearly represent a wealth of knowledge regarding the past. But the problem (presented by Henige as merely a matter of the purity of facts) is that traditional African histories represent a different order of knowledge than that of the historiographies into which ethnohistorians transform them. To the purveyor of facts, this difference emerges merely as interference in the research process or what Jan Vansina refers to as "distortions that arise in the course of transmission" (1965:19). I contend that attempts to correct these distortions, to reduce the "impact of the informant's performing sense," constitute another kind of distortion. An epistemological sleight of hand takes place when traditional representations of the past are transfigured into components of academic historiography. Regarding this question as it arose in his work with the Iraqw of Tanzania, Robert Thornton (1980:158) cogently observed:

> The Iraqw way of thinking about the past is different from our own "historical" ways of thinking about it; and I will maintain that any attempt to force the Iraqw's "facts" about the past into a Western, historical way of thinking about the facts, is not merely

a translation of one language's speech about the past into another language's terms, but is a distortion of the way in which the Iraqw conceive of and communicate about the past.

Thornton goes on to criticize the selective collection of texts and facts on the basis of historiographic criteria for objectivity and causality, arguing that the imposition of sequentiality on texts obscures indigenous principles of ordering. His own analysis examines Iraqw epic texts in terms of the insights they provide into Iraqw notions of time. I concur with Thornton's argument that African epic performances derive from temporal concepts distinct from those employed in academic historiography. However, Thornton's analysis continues to depend on interpretation of texts alone. We must also consider the problems arising from the methodological extraction of "texts" from the performative activities in which they are embedded. This is more than a matter of "situating text in context." The logocentrism inherent in text-collecting, text-producing research effaces the cognitive salience of other dimensions of performance. The nonverbal evocation of music, the opacity of the mask, the somatic logic of dance: these constitute orders of knowledge that must be explicated on their own terms. The analytical privilege assigned by historiographers to "oral history" and its "texts" obscures the most fundamental aspects of indigenous knowledge and experience of the past and its significance. For Ohafia people, the music sound and principles of bodily presentation associated with iri agha are fundamental. They are the frame in which texts can come into being. Hence, while the texts may contain historical data (accounts of specific events), they are not simply strings of facts. They are sung amid drumming and dancing while ọfụfụ is performed and trophy heads are displayed. The totality of iri agha embodies the Ohafia sense of history itself: a traditional methodology arising from an indigenous episteme.

The academic historiographer's overriding concern with the verification and sequentiality of texts assumes a particular kind of relationship between the present and the past, one in which these are discrete entities that interact as subject and object. In this view, agency is located wholly in the present, the past existing only as inert facts: data to be compiled and analyzed. But this is only one of many ways in which humans relate to the past. I am not arguing a kind of opposition between "African systems of thought" and "Western" ones. The introduction of schools and literacy long ago exposed Ohafia to academic conceptions of the past. But these conceptions were not unfamiliar. The field of study in which specialists argue heatedly over the factual details of past events was easily recognizable as analogous to the debates of older men who evaluate variants of the war songs. Historiography is common to both the academy and to Ohafia traditional culture. On the other hand, the mechanisms employed in iri agha, while distinctly African in their aesthetic form, are not without correlates in most societies including Euro-American ones. In Paul Connerton's (1989) excellent book *How Societies Remember* he examines social memory as bodily knowledge drawing many of his examples from European political culture. The growing popularity of historic theme parks, war reenactments, and Renaissance festivals attests to the aptness of "living history" in American society. The problem is not the product of essential differences in "mentality." Rather, the distinction between the war dance and academic historiography is due to their very different agendas.

The war dance is what Certeau (1986:4) calls a "mechanism" constituting a particular distribution of the "space of memory" in which past and present are interpermeable.[18] This mechanism works by way of an aesthetic structuring of experience that recapitulates history even as it constitutes it. In *African Rhythm and African Sensibility,* John Chernoff emphasizes that interpretations of African aesthetics that approach performance from an objectifying perspective fail because "the aesthetic point of this exercise is not to reflect a reality which *stands behind* it but to ritualize a reality that is *within* it" (1979:38).[19] Without thoughtful elucidation of the mechanisms by which Africans construct their past the study of African historical genres merely reproduces the politics of postcolonial relations: the extraction of raw data to be processed, packaged, and marketed abroad. African history has its own vehicles for knowledge; and these remain alive, powerful, and useful for most Africans, including many who have embraced European language, education, and religion.

## Display of Power: The Visual Dimension
## of the War Dance

The war dance is led by a dancer carrying a headdress. In the past, when a warrior was celebrated either after returning from battle or at his burial, the headdress carried was *ite odo*.[20] This was a large pot, blackened with sacrificial blood, upon which were tied the prepared heads of particularly formidable victims.[21] Another type of headdress called *oyaya* was carried to honor men who had killed leopards or had performed other brave deeds that were considered to be acts equivalent to the taking of a human head. Oyaya is the headdress that is now generally associated with the war dance. It is a long board covered with leopard skin and bearing decorated skulls or carved wooden representations of heads. The oyaya is occasionally referred to as a "leopard board," killing a leopard being taken as a gloss for all acts considered equivalent to head-taking. Thus the heads on the oyaya signify that the act celebrated is not the actual taking of a head but the accomplishment of something that is to be *represented as a head*.

The heads on the oyaya are either decorated skulls or simulacra sculpted of wood. They bear leopard caps, eagle feathers, and ram manes—the signifiers of manhood, fierceness, and courage that also adorn the dancers. The greatness of the victor is dependent upon the greatness of the victim for validation. There is no glory in overpowering women, children, or weak men. To associate oneself with the leopard, the eagle, and the ram, one must have opponents of equal stature. Thus the heads on the oyaya must resemble brave warriors themselves if they are to represent the accomplishment of great deeds. The ite odo is now rarely seen though it is still carried for the burial of particularly prominent chiefs.[22] The skull-studded vessels are maintained but they have largely become relics of an earlier age. The leopard rack, however, is at the center of a vital living tradition. Now used to celebrate men who have succeeded in business and educational endeavors, it resonates as a key symbol of the relationship between traditional Ohafia culture and the endeavors faced by Ohafia men in the modern world. Scholars have long noted the importance of the leopard as a metaphor for human power in Africa. The relationship between these mighty predatory cats and human authority is

Fig. 4.   A war dancer with ǫyaya bearing heads made of
leather-covered skulls. *(Amaekpu Ohafia 1991)*

generally associated with the leopard's ferociousness and its ability to take human life (Ruel 1969:246; Henderson 1972:276–77). The cutlass of the accomplished Ohafia warrior was carried in a leopard-skin sheath. The *okpu agụ* or "leopard hat" was a knit wool cap of black, white, and red. While the caps were striped rather than spotted, the design was said to represent the patterns on the skin of leopards.[23]

In earlier times the color red could only be worn by men who had taken heads, and the caps were said to be dyed with the blood of human victims. The visual references of the leopard hat and cutlass sheath are trappings of a more immediate identification between war dancer and leopard, which is fully realized by leopard-like bodily comportment in the dance itself. When Ohafia people offer aesthetic evaluation of dancers, their bodily movements are often favorably compared to those of leopards. The notion that the greatest warriors are able to *become* leopards, or at least in some bodily sense acquire the strength, agility, and poise of these great animals, is common throughout the Cross River region.[24] This is more an aesthetic assessment than it is a "belief." The leopard embodies power that is both wild and refined. It is the quality of movement itself, as exquisitely graceful as it is lethal, that constitutes the identification between warrior and leopard. Thus, the feline poise of the war dancer does not merely symbolize the power of the leopard. It is an embodiment of that power, immediately present and undeniably manifest.

The war dancers wear long white ram's manes wrapped on their upper arms. The ram is considered stubborn and forceful in its actions and constitutes a metaphor for these traits in humans. But more importantly, the ram is the penultimate sacrificial animal, second only to a human. Of all the sacrificial animals, the ram "represents a man." This identification between rams and humans in relation to sacrifice is widespread in the region. Robin Horton has noted that in some pieces of Kalabari shrine art the human face motif is actually replaced by the skull of a ram. These, his informants told him, "are a sign of the things we have given to the spirit" (1965:29). Thus the virility embodied in the ram's mane is linked not only to the ram's character but to the ritual equivalence of a sacrificial ram to a human being. The ram's mane distinguishes it from ewes and lambs. Draped on the upper arms of the war dancer, the ram's mane enhances the display of his virility and marks him as one who, through his actions, has distinguished himself from women and boys.

The fish eagle is also frequently associated with power in West Africa. Ben-Amos suggests that, like the leopard, the eagle is associated with power due to its "taxonomic position." They are "rulers or lords" of their genera, and as predators they are capable of taking lives (1976:247). The Ohafia cite the eagle's method of striking quickly and unexpectedly as the trait that it holds in common with the traditional warrior. Leopard caps are now frequently seen on children and young men who have not "earned" the right to wear them. While they are still identified as war caps, the right to them is not as severely restricted as it once was. The eagle feather, however, is still regarded as the property of those men who have been awarded it on the basis of their accomplishments, and any man who attempts to wear a feather he has not earned will be forced to remove it and may possibly be fined. Of all the visual markers that distinguish the Ohafia warrior, the eagle's feather most directly indicates official sanction: it must be presented by decision of an elite cadre of elder warriors, and feathers acquired otherwise will quickly be taken from those who pretend to have earned the honor.

The war dance leader usually holds a small palm leaf in his mouth. The meaning of palm leaf symbolism has often puzzled Western observers (e.g., comments on Perham [1962] in Leith-Ross [1939:25]). Part of the problem has been due to the fact that the detailed terminology the Igbo language applies to varieties and parts of leaves becomes collapsed by the English gloss "palm leaf." The leaf in the mouth of the war dancer is *ọmụ,* the tiny shoot of a new palm leaf. Traditionally, when the elders of a village decided to go to war with another village they would send a strong and well-armed man to deliver an ọmụ to the village chief. The ọmụ, a common object in itself, in this context represented a declaration of war. The ọmụ in the lead dancer's mouth indicates this potential for war. Its position in the mouth also carried significance. I was told that the leaf is held between the lips to remind all that when men go to war they must move stealthily and not speak. Speech was kept to a minimum when warriors were on the move. For the most part, all communication was accomplished with drum signals.

## The First and Second Head

In Ohafia, as boys grow up they learn to have a particular kind of relationship with their bodies, one that links their sense of their masculinity with the ancestral traditions of Ohafia. When a baby boy cuts his first teeth the occasion is celebrated, and he is said to have "cut his first head."[25] This bodily transformation is the first in a series of events that are considered to be equivalent to head-taking. When he reaches the age of seven or eight his father will provide him with a bow and arrows. These he learns to use in contests with other boys, shooting at balls of rolled leaves or other targets. He develops his skill with the bow because he must eventually kill a small bird.[26] When this is accomplished he is said to have "cut his second head."[27] A celebration follows in which the boy ties the dead bird to the end of his bow and marches through the village proclaiming his victory and singing that his age-mates who have not killed birds are cowards. Those of his age-mates who have also "cut their second heads" will join him. One of the traditional songs of the *nnụnnụ mbụ* (first bird) rite has been recorded by K. A. Ume (1960:3–4).

> Who? Who shot and missed! It flew away!
> Who? Who shot and missed! It flew away!
> Came out and shot crab? It flew away!
> His crab had no feathers! It flew away!
> Perere pere ja! It flew away!
> Pere ja pe ja ja! It flew away![28]

His father will dress him in a fine wrapper, and the procession will travel through the village visiting his kinspeople who give him yams and small amounts of money. In many cases it is through this process that the young boy first comes to know his maternal relations, many of whom, by virtue of the dispersed residence of the maternal family, he may never have met. Hence, at the age of seven or eight the young boy constitutes, through this first act of manhood, a new social role for himself. It is a role that allows him to ally himself with the most able of his age-mates and to distinguish himself from the "cowards." He is allowed to dress in finery reserved for adults, and he becomes a person of interest to his maternal family, the people who will ultimately grant him land and livelihood.

Unlike the traditional rites of passage for girls that have largely passed out of practice, such as the celebration of first menses and "fattening house" confinement prior to marriage, the bird-killing rite for boys is still considered essential in Ohafia and neighboring regions.[29] I was told a story of an adult Abiriba man who asked a friend to come to his wedding but was refused. His friend reminded him that he had never taken a second head and therefore had no right to get married. The man armed himself with a traditional bow and went into the bush, emerging later with a tiny bird. He was paraded through the village in a great celebration, and his story has since become a modern legend.

Young boys confided in me that some now use the rubber slingshots that are available at local markets to kill the birds. These simple weapons have a much greater range and accuracy than the traditional bow.[30] But if they do acquire their birds in this manner they must keep it a secret. Elders insist that the boys must use the traditional bows, not because of the greater test of skill, but, as one man explained, "because we must not forget how to use the weapons that our ancestors used." This remark should not be dismissed as mere nostalgia. It is an expression of the fact that, in marking this step in the transition from childhood to manhood, it is not the killing that is important but the production and reproduction of a particular bodily praxis, one rooted in ancestral tradition. Sometimes, enthusiastic boys raise their own war dance, complete with a small ọyaya. In Ohafia it is not enough to remember the stories of warriors of the past. Various rites and performances are specifically aimed at a somatic transmission of the knowledge of the Ohafia warrior. Whether this knowledge is embodied in aesthetically structured performance such as the war dance or in ceremonial constraints such as the sanctions surrounding the nnụnnụ mbụ rite, the bodily aspects of traditional practices are considered crucial.

Fig. 5.　A small boy dressed as a warrior. The chalk on his
eyes indicates that his paternal kinsmen are dibịa. *(Akanu
Ohafia 1989)*

## "Now We Take Degrees"

The war dance has changed considerably in the past century. Vocalists, once limited by the power of their own voices, can now employ amplification systems and fill the village commons with their resounding words. War dance troupes from Ohafia travel to distant cities to compete in state-sponsored "traditional cultural festivals." Recordings of the war dance, produced in studio environments, are available commercially. When I told people in other areas of Nigeria that I was living in Ohafia they consistently mentioned the war dancers as their referent for Ohafia. As a nationally performed music, the war dance has become an icon of Ohafia's ethnic identity within the ethnically diverse state of Nigeria.

While the age of head-taking is gone, modern markers of achievement serve equally well as tokens of proven courage and affirmed manhood. New signs have become structurally equivalent to "heads," worthy of celebration just as, in the past, the hunter who killed a leopard was celebrated as having "taken a head." The war dance is about achievement by way of appropriation of power and incorporation of the *other.* The head continues to stand as a resonant symbol of this achievement, but the actions that constitute the appropriation of power have transformed to embrace the structures and relations of modernity: the corporation, the academy, the state. Hence, the academic degree and the Mercedes-Benz are "heads" that, when brought home, establish the passage to full adulthood and status as a local hero, and they are often referred to as such.

Though the role traditionally played by war in establishing masculinity and associated social privileges was fundamental in Ohafia society, the end of the internecine wars of the nineteenth century did not result in a crisis in masculine identity. Rather, the institutions, values, dispositions, and expressive culture associated with the warrior hero tradition were transferred to a new context, that of achievement in the fields of endeavor established by the colonial powers. In conversations Ohafia men often explained to me, "In those days we went out and brought back heads. Now we bring back degrees." This transmigration of symbolic markers revealed an essential truth about the notion of achievement in the Ohafia context.

Fig. 6.   A dibịa and his son arrive at a festival on a motorcycle. Note that the handlebars are adorned with ram's mane
in much the same manner that war dancers adorn their arms.
*(Akanu Ohafia 1989)*

Underlying the practice of head-taking was a fundamental logic of
incorporation of the *other* and the acquisition of power inherent in
such an act. The process of attaining social recognition as a man of
achievement required a *going out* into the realm beyond the limits of
the familiar Ohafia world. It meant confronting the unknown, pre-
vailing against alien forces and conquering them on their own
ground. Returning with the head completed the act of incorporation.[31] The head stood as a resonant symbol of this accomplished
act, and thus a "celebration of the head" was a celebration of manhood itself.

   The war dance anchors the experience of postcolonial life in
Ohafia in a tradition of values based in a continuity of community,
family, and personhood. Many Ohafia people live abroad or in Lagos, Aba, Enugu, Calabar, Port Harcourt, and numerous other metro-
politan areas in Nigeria. These are "hard places" where many are

known to have failed. When they return from their long sojourns with the spoils of their achievements attesting to their success, they are celebrated. The identity realized here is not in the things themselves but in the all-important action of *returning* with them. Those who stay in the city and lose contact with their natal villages are referred to as "lost," as were the warriors who failed to return from battle. Material rewards are not enough to constitute an authentic Ohafia identity. The sojourn must be completed. The warrior must return, be celebrated, meet his ancestors, and join in the community of heroes. This sentiment is embodied in an Ohafia song that reminds mothers:

Mother who gives birth to a son, don't rejoice
until we have returned from war.
War is the difficult thing.

In the early twentieth century this song was transformed to embrace the new demands of the colonial order. The British employed many young Ohafia men to construct a railroad line to Port Harcourt. At that time, Port Harcourt was a center of British activity and was known in Ohafia as *ugwu ọcha,* or "hill of the white men." The new song expressed a new challenge and a traditional sentiment.

Mother who gives birth to a son, don't rejoice
until we have returned from ugwu ọcha.
Ugwu ọcha is a difficult place. (Agara 1991:17-A-00)

Through adaptation of the warrior tradition, the war dance provides a continuity with the past that circumvents the upheavals and social changes that have characterized the last century by appropriating these new elements. It is an embodiment of Ohafia identity that, faced with the transforming influences of consumer culture, religious conversion, and literacy, refuses to succumb and instead *incorporates* these elements like so many skulls adorning the shrine of a victorious people.

Each performance of the war dance is initiated by an offering of libations to the ancestors. They are called to come, to share the drink, and to join with the living in celebration of Ohafia's heroes, past and present. This action clears the way for the subsequent events and delineates a space in which the boundaries between the living and the dead, the past and the present, become permeable. This manipulation of time consciousness is fundamental to the experiential dimensions of the war dance. Through aesthetically framed enactments of past events and ancestral heroes, the war dance constitutes a collective experience that extends through time, linking the living to their predecessors. The term *history* fails to fully convey this sense of community unfolding through time. It is an experience of transtemporal communitas that is at the core of the war dance experience and ultimately of what it means to be Ndi Ohafia (Ohafia people). The collective community that participates in the creation of the war dance includes the living *and* the dead; for without the ancestors there would be no community with which to identify.

This presence of ancestors is not a "supernatural" notion. Rather, it is an empirically experienced glimpse of a social reality extending through time over many generations and thus normally outside of the mundane experience of present time consciousness. The war dance is simultaneously the celebration of a person's position within the community and the individual's role in defining the social grounds that constitute that community. For this reason it is a mechanism of change as well as one of continuity. Particular individuals are able to rise to prominence—those who have proven adept in the incorporation of power from external sources. In present-day Ohafia this may mean becoming a successful lawyer, accountant, physician, or teacher, but it also means maintaining relations with one's natal community and sharing one's wealth and success with others. Thus a hero must prove himself to be a master of both continuity *and* change. "Greatness," however, rarely goes uncontested. One family's hero may be scorned by others. On one occasion I was sitting with a group of men in Akanu when a young man came to announce the death of an elder who was matrilineally related to the owner of the house in which we were meeting. The messenger, who was a paternal relative of the deceased, invited all to join in (and contribute money to) the burial proceedings for the recently departed "hero." When the visitor was gone the man of the house scoffed at the notion that the late man was a hero, referring to several instances when he had avoided his responsibilities to his matrilineal kinspeople. Greatness depends upon relative positions in the social scheme. It is also strategic: the paternal kinspeople had more prestige to gain from a big ceremony than did the skeptical matrilineal relative. Ultimately, the hero is a product of both his own actions and the interests and actions of his kinspeople.

The Ohafia war dance does more than express or reproduce Ohafia notions of ethnicity, gender, and history. It structures a lived experience of these, and in doing so it becomes the very means of producing them. The Ohafia warrior tradition is a social production as well as a social fact. In Ohafia as elsewhere, the performance arts embody this constitutive process. They create a nexus at which the individual and the collective intersect. It is at this nexus of the part and the whole, the person and society, identity and history, creator and created, that social forms emerge and can be transformed. Such a view accounts for the fact that the war dance has retained currency in Ohafia even though head-taking, its putative object, is no longer practiced. The dance itself has proven to be more vital than the practice it originally commemorated, the act of celebration more definitive than the act celebrated.

CHAPTER 4

# The Eagle Warriors

In the nineteenth century the vast region east of Lagos, which became known to the British as the Oil Rivers Protectorate, was a dangerous place. Internecine warfare was rife, stimulated to unprecedented levels by the slave trade and its lucrative demand for captives. In 1807 the British decreed the abolition of slave trading, and by the mid-century external demand for slaves was nearly nonexistent. However, the blockade on the coast had unanticipated consequences. The slave trade was a centuries-old enterprise that had become such an integral part of the economy of the region that British suppression failed to eliminate slave acquisition activities. Reduced external demand produced a glut of slaves on the market, depressing prices and greatly expanding the internal market. The "legitimate" trade in palm oil with which the British hoped to replace the slave economy became largely dependent upon slave labor (Afigbo 1981:241). Lowered slave prices also had other, more macabre consequences. The practice of human sacrifice at burials, which had previously been used to honor kings, became widespread. The greater availability of cheap slaves allowed human sacrifice to become a common occurrence among secret societies and at the burials of minor chiefs (241–42).[1] When Ohafia people speak of "those days" they tell stories of the abduction of children sent to fetch water and the risk of traveling to market in a village where you were not well known. It was a time of persistent danger and relentless ongoing warfare.

The ancestral fathers of the Ohafia people were renowned as mighty and ruthless warriors. Traditionally, men who failed to distinguish themselves by bringing home a human head from battle found themselves utterly marginalized in their communities. Spurned by potential wives, barred from active participation in age-grade activities, and branded *ụjọ* meaning "coward," the unaccomplished man was considered to have failed to establish his masculinity and would be referred to as a "woman in the skin of a man." In addition to the militant character of the tradition of Ohafia manhood, Elizabeth Isichei (1976:82) has observed that the Ohafia came with "peace and a sword." She notes that warfare abroad was balanced by a highly developed art of peaceful diplomacy at home. While they occasionally engaged in border conflicts with their neighbors (stories of skirmishes between different villages within Ohafia are still recalled with relish whenever petty conflicts arise) local disputes were more often settled by peaceful means. For the Ohafia, the control of aggressive violence within their own sphere was paramount. As Isichei notes:

> It is much to the credit of the Ohafia that they did not obtain these heads by kidnapping stray travellers. They obtained them only in a legitimate war—crossing the length and breadth of Igboland, if necessary, in search of such a war. (82)

The maintenance of peace within Ohafia was essential because of the daily need for safe passage between its various constituent villages, which extended over 100 square miles. Agricultural land was held matrilineally but residence after marriage was virilocal. Thus, a family's farms might be spread far and wide, often a great distance from their village of residence.[2] The traditional system of staggered market days, which dictated that separate villages must hold their markets on different days, also encouraged frequent travel to other villages for the exchange of goods.

The primary symbol of peace in Ohafia was chalk (*nzụ*). It is said that its white color represents "whiteness of heart" (*obi dị ọcha*) or good intentions. Any trusted male guest in a village was always offered chalk in a wooden bowl by his host, and this he would rub on the back of his wrist. A woman would rub it on her belly where it was said to enhance the fertility of her womb, or, if she had a baby, on her chest above her breasts. Anyone suspicious of the person's intentions in the village would ask who had presented them with chalk. If the sponsor proved to be genuine they were thus protected. This use of chalk was once widely practiced in Igboland, but in most areas it has fallen from use. The Ohafia, however, still consider offering chalk to guests to be an important gesture of hospitality.

Perhaps the single most important institution for assuring safe passage for travelers who ventured into the non-Igbo regions south of Ohafia was the Ekpe society. The membership of Ekpe (Egbo in some dialects) extended to many different ethnic groups including Efik, Ekoi, Igbo, and Ibibio. The word *ekpe* means "leopard" in Efik, and leopard symbolism is prevalent in the iconography. Members go through various levels of initiation and at each stage are instructed in the meaning and deployment of a repertoire of secret signs or *nsibidi* (*nsibiri* in Ohafia). These signs come in the form of gestures and manners of bodily comportment as well as written hieroglyphic representations. Early anthropologists (Talbot, Blackwood) were fascinated by written nsibidi because of the implications this had for assumptions about written language in West Africa. This interest, however, led them to ignore the performative/gestural manifestations of nsibidi that were the primary form to which the written symbols made reference. This system of secret gestures constituted a sign language that allowed members who spoke different languages to communicate and, most importantly, to establish their status as Ekpe initiates, which guaranteed them safe passage. High initiation costs restricted membership to wealthy traders who were thus able to travel freely in regions where others feared to tread. The society had its own courts, and those who threatened, harmed, or stole from the membership were dealt with harshly. The trappings of secrecy and supernatural awe inspired by the arcane symbols and dancing masquerades only enhanced the threat of very real jural sanction that protected Ekpe members and their trade monopoly.

Another important system of peace maintenance in Ohafia and neighboring areas was a ritual process called *igbandu̞*. This rite bound two individuals by oath, each swearing never to take any action that would result in the death of the other. It was believed that failure to keep the oath would result in inevitable death for the oath breaker. When conflicts over land boundaries or wrongful actions led to violence, the potential for an escalation of the conflict was usually contained by bringing the disputants before the elders of both villages and compelling them to establish i̞gbandu̞.[3] I̞gbandu̞ was used not only to maintain peace between villages but in a wide range of personal disputes, including conflicts between cowives. It was also used to establish dependable business relations and safe travel. U. I. Ukwu (1967:650) observed that traders and other travelers often re- lied on a succession of ịgbandụ relationships to assure safe passage over long distances. An ịgbandụ host would escort them to the next village where the next ịgbandụ host would assume responsibility.

## In Pursuit of Glory

Most of the battles fought by the Ohafia were waged on behalf of the Aro people located just south of Ohafia. It is difficult to establish when the Ohafia began providing military assistance to the Aro. While the war dance epics recall many battles, most of the songs sung today refer to battles that occurred late in the nineteenth cen- tury. However, the shallow time depth of the war epics does not necessarily mean that the warrior tradition was a recent occurrence. As Isichei has observed:

> The wars fought in the 1890s were the last of their kind, and thus appear as unique and unforgettable. Their uniqueness pre- serves all the attendant details, like a fly in amber. They are remembered, not because they were the most important wars, but because they were the last. (1976:75)

In the centuries prior to the colonial period the Aro established settlements over a wide region of southeastern Nigeria between the Cross River and the Niger. The original expansion of Aro influ- ence may have been accomplished with the military support of the Ohafia or, as Afigbo has suggested (1981:207), it may have developed slowly by way of trade relationships and other peaceful means. In either case, it is clear that by the beginning of the nineteenth cen- tury the Aro were well established and were expanding their domain and their wealth by way of military operations manned primarily by mercenary troops from Ohafia and their neighbors, the Abam and the Edda (Isichei 1973:35).[4] The Aro took possession of conquered villages, pillaged for booty, and acquired slaves that they traded southward to the coastal Efik. During this period of expansion they profited greatly from plunder and slave trade. Though no formal dominion in the region was established, the Aro were powerful, wealthy, and politically influential. Ohafia people, however, saw little of the bounty. Their primary interest in the wars was the acquisition of human heads and the prestige and social power that these heads represented within Ohafia society. In fact, many Ohafia people argue that the term *mercenary* should not be applied to these soldiers whose only interest was the glory gained in victory. Nsugbe supports the opinion that Ohafia profited little from warfare, noting that while Ohafia probably gained slaves and food from the raids they conducted, there is little evidence that they acquired any of the European trade goods that were commonly exchanged in the south (1974:31–32). Isichei cites the recollections of Oji Kalu Oji who insisted that the tribute offered to the Ohafia for participation in the raids went to sponsor the rituals conducted to prepare for battle (1976:82).

The traditional Ohafia economy depended largely on women's agricultural labor. Men cleared land, planted yams, and gathered palm fruits and wine. While men engaged in specializations other than soldiering, such as hunting, fishing, traditional medicine, and trading of nonagricultural goods, women's day-to-day agricultural labor and food marketing activities formed the basis of subsistence production and consumption. While the war activities of men were not motivated by direct economic reward, the successful hero was able to marry many wives and thus control the products of their labor. In addition, the recognized warrior could dominate in the affairs of both his maternal and paternal lineages and monopolize land usage rights. Hence, head-taking accrued symbolic capital that was essential for men's social and economic survival in Ohafia.

Ohafia traditions recall attacks upon villages throughout the length and breadth of Igboland. The war songs record defeats as well as victories. Their attack upon Nteje northeast of Onitsha was a bitter loss for Ohafia (Arua 1951:11–12). The village of Nteje, hammered by repeated attacks by its neighbors at Awkuzu and earlier raids by the Aro, had become a walled citadel surrounded by watchtowers and proved invincible (Isichei 1976:84). But the songs record many victories, some at villages whose exact locations can no longer be determined because the wars devastated them completely. Ukpati, which was probably north of present-day Enugu, is an example (Arua 1951:11). Most of the activity took place far from Ohafia in the Onitsha area and the Anambra River valley where, according to Isichei, "they wreaked great havoc" (1976:84).

The Ohafia man maintained two faces. The outward-looking face, that which regarded the outside world of the *other*, was that of a ruthless and bloodthirsty warrior whose desire for heads overrode any concern for politics or personal gain. The inward-looking face, that which regarded his own domain of domestic affairs, was that of a negotiator, peacemaker, husband, and father.

## The Aro and the British

When the Royal Niger Company of Great Britain began to success-fully monopolize external trade from the coast of Southern Nigeria in the nineteenth century, a different order of historical conscious-ness forced its way into the Nigerian hinterland. A European para-digm of history grounded in the Victorian notion of progress was set in motion through the media of company agents and missionaries, trade policies and schools. It was a view of history and intergroup relations fundamentally distinct from that of the Ohafia.

The agents of colonialism saw the expansion and dominance of Africa by European peoples as an inevitable unfolding of a social evolutionary process. Indeed, many writers took the eventual extinc-tion of the African races to be a foregone conclusion.[5] Even those who did not predict extinction assumed that "civilization" would rapidly eradicate all traces of traditional African culture. This was viewed simultaneously as a natural and inevitable process and as the specific mission of the European races: the "white man's burden." The colo-nial writers of the period decry the "brutish barbarism" of the people of the region. Likewise, indigenous accounts of early contacts express a stunned incredulity as they recall indiscriminate massacres and the arrogant violence of colonial officials. In fact, there were martial societies on both sides of the encounter. But their principles of war and logics of violence were of two incommensurable orders.

The Ohafia were far removed from the coast, and their encounter with colonial "history" came only with the dawning of the twentieth century. While Lagos had been a British colony since 1861, the hinterlands of Southern Nigeria were still largely independent of British influence at the turn of the century. Centralized indigenous political structures, which had facilitated colonial control of the protectorates at Lagos and in northern Nigeria, were not present in the southeastern region. Instead, hundreds of autonomous communities presented a very different kind of problem. The British policy of indirect rule was intended to preserve indigenous leadership, and intervention by the British advisers was officially restricted to limitation of internecine warfare, reduction of tyranny and corruption, suppression of the slave trade, and control of trade with the French protectorates (Wiedner 1964:253–55). These limitations did not prevent them from challenging the loosely defined oligarchy of the Aro whose primary activities in the region centered on warfare and slave trade.

At the same time, the British presence was slowly moving inland. The Church Missionary Society (CMS) made inroads up the Cross River and by 1888 had missions as far north as Ikot-Ana over a hundred miles north of Calabar (Afigbo 1981:243).[6] With the transfer of administration from the Royal Niger Company in 1891, the British designated the vast area east of Lagos as the "Oil Rivers Protectorate."[7] The Protectorate came under the control of Sir Ralph MacDonald who immediately initiated a program to disengage communities from economic relations with the Aro in an attempt to limit their influence.

For both the Protectorate and the missions, the primary symbol of persisting Aro hegemony was the "Long Juju." More properly known in Igbo as *Ibin Ukpabi,* the Long Juju was an oracular shrine (*arụnsi*) that traditionally served as the ultimate arbiter in legal disputes in the region. The British recognized that the shrine was a symbol of Aro political power, and they claimed that its priests played a pivotal role in the slave trade. In fact, while the Long Juju's "victims," that is, litigants who were found guilty and were "eaten" by the oracle, soon found themselves on the block at the slave markets in

Calabar and Opobo, they only represented a minuscule portion of the overall market in slaves.

The destruction of the Long Juju loomed large in the mind of the high commissioner of the Protectorate, Sir Ralph Moor. In 1899 Moor, in a memo to the undersecretary of state, proposed a military expedition of 87 officers, 1,550 men and 2,100 carriers into the hinterlands (Nwabara 1977:100). Among the express purposes of the expedition were "to abolish the slave trade . . . to abolish the fetish of the Aros known as the Long Ju-ju . . . to open up the whole of Ibo country lying between the Cross River and the Niger to civilisation and trade" (100). However, G. I. Jones, who acted as the district officer in Bende until 1946, questioned the Protectorate's good faith in their contention that the destruction of the "fraudulent fetish" of the Aro would assist in bringing the slave trade under control: "The objectives outlined in the correspondence read more like a propaganda exercise intended to impress informed British public opinion and its parliament" (1988:130). Jones observed that the actual purpose of the military expedition was to gain political control of the people in the region between Bende and the coast, a heterogeneous population that seemed singularly unsuited to control by way of "indirect rule" (132).

When the Aro became aware of the preparations for the invasion they hastened to move first. The Aro, who considered the British to be the enemy of the Igbo people, were outraged that the village of Obegu was assisting the Protectorate in its plans for assault on Aro Chukwu. They attacked Obegu with a large battalion of fighters.[8] Caught unawares, Obegu was overwhelmed, and the massacre left some 400 villagers dead. In response, Lieutenant-Colonel A. F. Montanaro, the commanding officer of the "Aro Field Force," moved his columns into action (Nwabara 1977:104).

The expedition was massive in comparison to earlier military excursions in the region. For fifteen months "columns crossed and recrossed southern Igboland and Ibibioland" (Isichei 1976:128). Under the command of Officer Mackenzie one column of troops proceeded up the Cross River. Arua (1951:14) records that Mackenzie was guided by two sons of Ohafia, Eke Kalu of Amaekpu and Ationu of Ama Ngwu. However, as Kalu tells it, he traveled from Calabar on his own in a canoe (1954:7).[9] In either case, his goal was to warn his countrymen of the imminent invasion.

> I realised that my people, the famous and dreaded hordes of ancient Ohafia, the lions of the jungle, the proud and gallant sons of Uduma Ezema the Great, would challenge the soldiers. I realised too that though their military tactics might surpass that of the R.W.A.F.F., yet their weapons, dane-guns[10] and matchets, were incomparable to the rifles and devastating machine guns of the soldiers. (7)

The troops traveled north on the river to a point near Afikpo. Then moving southward by land they entered Ohafia. They found a war already in progress between the village of Okagwe and the Edda to the north. At first the expedition thought they were a resistance force, but the warriors scattered when they saw the British soldiers. The guides traveled ahead, warning the Ohafia villagers of the futility of resisting British firepower, and as a result Ohafia submitted with little resistance. However, indigenous accounts vary widely regarding the taking of Ohafia. Arua writes that after a bloodless seizure of Ebem, the troops found two headless bodies on the road and returned to the village "to open fire on mere suspects" (1951:16). Kalu records that after refusing to fetch water for the soldiers an Ebem man (Idika Echeme) shot at the British troops who responded by opening fire indiscriminately and "houses and trees began to fall from the impact of cannon balls" (1954:8). Ndukwe writes that the expedition met with "heavy resistance" at Ebem and that a British officer was killed (1971:24).[11] It is clear that some sort of altercation took place in Ebem and that villagers were massacred. The inconsistency of accounts based on the memories of Ohafia witnesses underscores the fundamental irrationality of the British actions to Ohafia observers. The Ohafia, whose warriors thought nothing of decapitating the hapless defenders of the villages they attacked, had a clearly defined sense of where, when, and how violence was appropriately executed. This original encounter, in which British troops fired upon citizens gathered in the village *ogo* (commons), remains, for the Ohafia, a symbol of the basic inhumanity of the colonial regime.

The bitter poignancy of this moment was captured by the Ohafia historian Arua when he wrote:

> Ohafia, the land of the eagle warriors, the town where only the strongest could find pleasure, the country of the invincible soldiers had been overrun by British Forces whose number never exceeded our modern battalion of infantry. (1951:16–17)

With Ohafia "pacified," the troops proceeded to Arochukwu and joined Montanaro's column. The battle at Arochukwu was prolonged despite a liberal use of machine guns. Montanaro later wrote, "The enemy has shown himself to be a most persistent and dogged foe, and I . . . had no idea that savages could make such a stand" (Nwabara 1977:105).

The Long Juju was located and destroyed with dynamite. Attempts to arrest the priests were largely unsuccessful, but they were driven into hiding and were never able to regain the overt control they once enjoyed. As with other arụnsi that were destroyed by government and church authorities, *Ibin Ukpabi* continued to function covertly. However, after the arrival of the British it rapidly became apparent to the Ohafia that the reign of the Aro was over and with it the regional conflicts that had provided them with the means to acquire heads. A new center of authority had been established, and the Ohafia rapidly began to adapt to the British presence. However, the Ohafia people did not merely "evolve" by assimilating European characteristics as Victorian theorists had imagined. They *incorporated* the new order into their traditional worldview. While manly attainment could no longer be measured in heads, the new system of authority brought with it other domains of achievement: Christian institutions, education, and international commerce. These, the Ohafia soon reasoned, were their new measures of power.

## The New Order of Power

Within a decade of the Aro expedition the British presence was well established in Ohafia. In 1906 a "native court" was set up by the administration in the village of Ebem. In 1912 a Scottish Free Presbyterian missionary named Robert Collins established a school in the same village. Interest in the mission school grew rapidly, and by 1924 four other Ohafia villages had established their own schools (Ume 1960:20). G. I. Jones, who was a district officer for the colonial government in that region, suggested that Ohafia accepted the schools more rapidly than the neighboring Abam because they did not have the boys' initiation societies that occupied Abam youths.[12] While Abam was as active in war as Ohafia, Ohafia put more stress on warfare as the primary initiatory passage into manhood.

Despite the relatively rapid growth of the mission schools, there was initial resistance to mission education. The first missions served as sanctuaries for the mothers of twins and their despised offspring. Fear of contamination by "twin mothers" led many to avoid the schools and churches. Various practices were employed to "encourage" participation in the schools. Colonial agents and missionaries conscripted children, pressuring family patriarchs to send at least one child to the school. Several old chiefs who had been among the first to rise in prominence by way of literacy laughed as they told me that their fathers had chosen them to send to school because they were the laziest of their siblings and their fathers considered them worthless for farm work. Other children made the choice themselves. Elder O. Eke of Amaekpu told me this story of his own decision to attend school:

If there is any piece of work in the village the age-grades who are supposed to do the job will be named through a town crier. So it happened that my age-grade was to be supplying water to the native court officials. That piece of work was to be done every four days, preferably upon the market day of the village people. . . .[13] Every *Afọ* it will be Amaekpu, this is my village: two age-grades will supply water to court officials. Then on every *Nkwọ* Ebem will give their own. On *Eke,* Elu. On *Orie* it will be Mbaga. So there will be no day when water service is not carried out. On one occasion it happened that when we lined out our pots of water . . . the court messenger who came to distribute this observed a maggot in one of the pots. . . . We were all surprised! Why should this thing be found in a pot of water? So they ordered every water brought to be thrown out. And then we were all flogged, everyone, irrespective of in whose pot it was found. Everybody flogged because it seemed to them that we brought stored rain water. So they . . . sent [us] again to the spring to get fresh water. That we did. So, that punishment by flogging me grieved me to the core. As I was returning I was thinking of this: why should these people flog me? Supposing I go to school? Then one mind said: if you go to school they will flog you. And one mind asked me: if they flog me they will teach me. But these people who flogged me today, did they teach me anything? So I must go to school because . . . school children do not join the age-grades in bringing this water. Only those who do not go to school do the service. School pupils are exempted from doing this because they are in school. So 20th August, 1923, I went to school. (Eke 1990:13-B-01)[14]

In time, other advantages of attending school became apparent. School graduates found work as teachers, mission clerks, and government employees and thus had means to attain wealth and power that were unavailable to the illiterate. By the 1940s the Ohafia people had embraced mission education aggressively. Raised in a tradition that valued achievement and prestige, they assessed the rules of the new political order and quickly developed strategies to use them to their advantage. Specifically, literacy and school certificates were identified as powerful tools for social advancement. The grandchildren of warriors became a new generation of scholars, lawyers, medical doctors, and entrepreneurs.

Regardless of whether heads or degrees were the mark of distinction the underlying paradigm defining achievement remained. To prove themselves men had to leave the village and venture into the wider world with all of its dangers and challenges. Those who never returned were considered "lost." Those who never left the village or who returned without distinction had little power in village affairs. But when a man returned having made his mark in the world, with conspicuous wealth, fine clothes, a car, and many gifts for his kins-people, he was celebrated in the traditional Ohafia manner, with a performance of the war dance.

## Stubborn Men

It would appear that when the dominance of the Aro was displaced by the British presence, head-taking became a symbolic token of a particular way of relating to the world, a symbol of aggressive achievement that was not inherently linked to war or killing. But this transmutation of meaning required a break in generations: a new generation of Ohafia males. Men trained in war could not simply transform themselves into attentive schoolboys. There were many stories of the "stubborn men" of the interim period, those who continued to face the world with a cutlass rather than a pen. One such man was Nna Ajike of Akanu.

In the 1930s the roads between the villages of Ohafia were little more than narrow paths through the bush. Ajike hid along these paths and ambushed strangers who passed.[15] Finally, two of his victims, a trader and his money carrier, escaped, leaving Ajike with a bleeding head-wound. The trader reported the attack to the colonial office in Bende, and court messengers, who functioned as police, were sent to find Ajike. Ajike went into hiding in Akanu, but the residents, fearing retribution from the court officials, conducted a manhunt.

The Akanu elders sent an age-grade to tap palm wine for the whole village and raised the Èkpè dance. They knew that Ajike was a great Èkpè dancer and that he could not resist its compelling rhythms. Methodically proceeding through the village, they stopped and performed at each commons singing: "Ajike, why don't you join us! We are looking for you! Come out! This is your dance!" "What are you waiting for?" and the like. Ajike's friend, who was protecting him, begged him not to expose himself because the wound on his head would prove that he was the criminal that the court sought. But Ajike ran out anyway, and it is said that he danced magnificently, proclaiming as he did that even if he was to die, if he could dance this last dance he would be satisfied. Ajike was finally turned over to the authorities. He was sent to work in a leper colony and returned to Akanu many years later much to the surprise of his relatives who believed that he had been hanged[16] (Kalu 1991a:07-A-02).

Countless other tales of stubborn men were told. The tradition that a man needed to be buried with skulls attesting to his accomplishments in life if he was to join the ancestral fathers is said to have been responsible for some of the latter-day instances of head-taking. But in time stubborn men became rarer, and, like Ajike's, their stories acquired the character of folktales. In Ohafia, the head was a metonym of masculine personhood, in particular, the power and authority of great men. The imposed order of the colonial state redefined the terms upon which masculine power could be based. The creation of structural equivalency between trophy heads and university degrees, automobiles, or other modern markers of success was implemented by way of performative means, particularly through the performance of the war dance. This process of transposition was clear in the following statement by war dance vocalist Ogba Kalu as recorded by Azuonye:

> Today, head-hunting is out of fashion, But if you grow rich or become highly educated, especially if you go to the white man's land and return with your car and immense knowledge, we would naturally perform [*iri agha*] for you. The point is that by doing these things, you have won your own battle honours. Passing your examinations well and bringing home the white man's money: these are the prevailing kinds of war we have today. If you achieve these, they are counted for you as your own battle honours. The same is true of building a big house, one that is truly imposing. People will say (on seeing it): your money is your battle trophy. On the day such a house is opened, we would normally perform for you, for by building it, you have won your own head in battle, for things of this kind are the only kind of head-hunting that exists in our present-day culture. (Azuonye 1974:387)

## Strategic Atavisms

In earlier times, when a man returned with a trophy head he first went to the chief of the warriors (*Eze Ite Odo*) who would verify and acknowledge his claims. Then he would go to the *ikoro ukwu*, the big slit drum in the village center. The *Eze Ikoro,* or priest of the *ikoro,* would call his praises on the big drum, and the head would be prepared. The head was roasted and only the skull preserved. This was washed and treated in a tincture of herbs. The man was considered to be dangerous and was isolated from others until a ceremony called *ịgba ọgbụgba agha,* or war cleansing, was performed. This was done because "his hands were said to be stained with blood" (Ume 1960:16). A. K. Ume describes this ceremony in his book *Ohafia d'Ike N'Agha:*

> On the day of the ceremony the skull was prepared for presentation. It was painted with *ufie* and *odo* and copper rings were affixed to each side. During the ceremony the man's wife held the skull by these rings while the man rubbed himself with *ufie* and *odo.* He then carried a large clay pot called *"nja"* used to wash his hands, legs, and face. Members of his age-grade and friends and relations would accompany him to the ritual site prepared for the war cleansing ceremony. Every village in Ohafia has its own ritual site.
>
> The man led the procession to the ritual site while others followed behind. Women played their *aja,* singing and dancing as they moved along. The war dance was played and the horn player could be heard calling the man by praise names. The man, painted in red and yellow, wearing his leopard cap with a white eagle feather was admired by all. He had become a real man of bravery and strength, and boys who saw the procession would want to go to war someday and bring home a head.
>
> On arrival at the ritual site the procession would stop and the music would cease. The man entered the ritual site alone with the clay pot full of water. Everybody watched him as he washed his face, legs, and hands. After washing he held the pot up and then let it drop to the ground where it would break into pieces. As the pot shattered everybody shouted for joy because the man had successfully cleansed himself of the taint of killing. They returned to the village playing the war dance and the women continued to play *aja* and sing the man's praises. The music and dancing would continue throughout the day into the night. (16–17)[17]

There is an ambiguity at the heart of Ohafia manhood that must comprehend both the compassionate act of generosity and the ruthless act of war. Both kinship and violence have their proper frames. Michelle Rosaldo observes a similar ambiguity in regard to Ilongot head-hunting. In the Ilongot case, as with the Ohafia, both violence and compassion are experienced as emanating from the "heart."

> What is clear in Ilongot talk of hearts is, in short, a sense of dialectic or dynamic tension between a state of sociality and one of opposition and withdrawal. . . . The two terms that are the subject of my text—*beya* and *liget*, 'knowledge' and 'passion'— capture well this tension between civility and unrestrained vitality, bespeaking the dependence of cooperative life and reasoned action upon potentially disruptive force. (1980:44)

The war cleansing rite constitutes a passage from the externally oriented relations of violence back into internally oriented relations of community. It creates the possibility of the coexistence of these radically different positions in relation to others. As warfare was suppressed, and education and commerce became the new arenas for advancement, the phrase "taking heads" came to refer to successfully mastering the new social order. While this order was imposed by British colonialists, its formalization was molded by indigenous mechanisms as much as by the constraints of colonial rule. As this new order evolved, the aggression of war became enfolded in the performance of the war dance and thus woven into the fabric of life: the past encapsulated as a model of the perseverance and courage required for success. The dance continued to celebrate achievement in a manner that preserved the knowledge, and thus the potential, of actual warriorhood. The act of decapitation, the habitus of the warrior, the will to face death, were embodied, not only as idiom, but as aesthetically framed and experienced performance.

The Biafran conflict (1967–79) turned the new order on its head. Most Igbo people I spoke to were reluctant to reflect upon this period. It was a time when the promise of prosperity that had exhilarated Nigerians after independence dissolved in a nightmare of unimaginable suffering. In such a moment the legacy of Ohafia warriors, scrupulously preserved in performance, had practical significance. The reservoir of history could only be tapped when it had not been reduced to abstracted texts—when it had been kept *alive* through embodied performance. The fact of modern warfare gave the lie to the myth of Progress underlying the colonial and missionary agenda. The same British nation that brought "peace" and "civilization" to the people of southeastern Nigeria ultimately put weapons of unimaginable powers of destruction into the hands of the Nigerian government, which opposed the independence of the Biafran state. This betrayal of progress exposed the limits of rationalized notions of temporality and opened the gates of history that, because of ritual access, had never been locked.

> During the problem in Nigeria [the Biafran war], the Ohafia man, actually used the opportunity to remind himself of what his forefathers used to be. And while he was very loyal to the country, as a fighter, at the same time he was actually renewing his records . . . some of us, during that time, used to be teachers. But at a time like that you forget about teaching, you forget about anything and become an Ohafia man on full stop.[18]

The great war arụnsi Ikwan in Elu again received sacrifice and was called upon for purposes it had not served in seven decades. The Ohafia fought in the conflict with the legendary ruthlessness of their forefathers. The ite odo was carried anew, and the traditional war cleansing ritual again had a meaningful role in mediating between the ideal of collective community and the reality of the disruptive forces of war. Ohafia people are quick to remember that Ohafia never fell during the war. When nearly all of the fledgling Biafran state had been overrun by federal soldiers, Ohafia remained inviolate. Nigerian troops entered Ohafia only after Biafra had officially surrendered. Many reasons for this could be argued, political, geographical, and tactical, but for the Ohafia, the explanation lies in the fear that the Ohafia have always inspired in their enemies.

## CHAPTER 5

# Rethinking Ancestors

Like many residents of rural areas of Africa, Ohafia people continue to maintain shrines for their ancestors, and ritual practices pertaining to ancestors remain an important aspect of daily life and agricultural activities. The fact that ancestors remain a vigorous element in the lives of Ohafia people, and, indeed, people in many rural communities in Africa, stands in stark contrast to the recent decline of interest in ancestors and ancestor-related practices among scholars of African culture and society. This divergence between cultural practice and scholarly interest is largely due to developments in Western scholarship quite unrelated to the relative importance of ancestors in the experience of African people. I will briefly outline these developments before turning to a discussion of my own findings.

Ancestors have long held an important place in anthropology. Spencer, Tylor, and Frazer all considered "ancestor worship" to constitute the definitive mark of "primitive religion." Regarded as such, much attention was given to these practices, and their interpretation was central to Victorian models of the evolution of religion and the evolution of society in general. In African ethnology, evolutionary concerns eventually gave way to functionalist models of African societies, but ancestors remained a key component in discussions of the maintenance of jural authority, land tenure systems, and segmentary social organization. The structural-functional theory of ancestors reached its logical culmination some two decades ago with Igor Kopytoff's article "Ancestors as Elders in Africa" (1971). In it he argued that Africans did not make significant distinctions between ancestors and living elders. According to Kopytoff, the question of whether a person in a position of political and jural authority was dead or alive was merely a preoccupation of Western academics and it held little relevance for the African. He attempted to support this rather startling proposition with linguistic evidence that Bantu terms used to refer to ancestors were identical to those used to denote living elders. By subsuming ritual sacrifice under the rubric of gift exchange, Kopytoff claimed that the "supernatural" element of ancestor rites was revealed to be a spurious residue of Western analytical bias.

Kopytoff's article appeared to challenge the entire history of theory regarding ancestors at an epistemological level. After its publication, his article was widely criticized. James Brain (1975) and Eugene Mendosa (1976) challenged both the relevance of his linguistic criteria and the validity of his interpretation of ritual practices. In spite of these criticisms (some of which I think were well founded), the article and the controversy surrounding it raised important issues. In particular, I think that Kopytoff's contention that Western scholars have exaggerated the "supernatural" nature of ancestors bears serious consideration. I would suggest, however, that while his argument appears to challenge the status quo at a fundamental level, it is actually an extreme statement of the structural-functional position. Among Kopytoff's critics only Victor Uchendu (1976:285) identified this dimension of Kopytoff's stance.

> In my view, this theory replaces "structural symbolism" with "structural realism" and, by equating the world of the descent group with the world of the ancestors, it asserts a "structural fusion" that represents the highest form of reductionism.

Uchendu (1976:295) observed that analyses that reduced the character of relations with ancestors to a structural role were particularly inadequate to deal with these practices among the Igbo people where ancestors were "both objects of honor and tools or agents which can be manipulated to achieve competitive goals." Unfortunately, while Uchendu's critique advocated a practice-based approach, he failed to follow through and instead moved to discuss Igbo cosmology.[1] While it was clearly Kopytoff's intention to revitalize the discourse on ancestors in Africa, his argument, entrenched as it was in a functionalist view of society, could not mark a turning point. Rather, it signaled that the anthropological tradition of explaining ancestor-related practices in terms of a jural model of social organization had reached a kind of theoretical cul-de-sac.

A second, closely related development contributing to the stagnation of scholarly interest in ancestors was the fact that lineage theory, to which the discourse on ancestors had been inextricably linked, was coming under increased scrutiny (Karp 1978; Van Leynseele 1979; Kuper 1982a). The debate surrounding lineage analysis was summarized in Adam Kuper's article "Lineage Theory: A Critical Retrospect" (1982b). Kuper's argument was cogent if heavy-handed. Tracing lineage theory through its origins in Victorian kinship theory (Maine 1870; Morgan 1877) Kuper identified the crystallization of lineage theory in the works of Evans-Pritchard (1940a, 1940b, 1945, 1951) and Fortes (1945, 1949a, 1949b, 1953). After briefly discussing the impact of Lévi-Strauss's alliance theory and Leach's transactional analysis, Kuper argued that lineage theory ultimately succumbed on the ethnographic battlefields of New Guinea. Kuper (1982b:90) cites Strathern who "pursued the ideological meanings of claims that neighbors are 'brothers,' and revealed a complex interpretation of ideas, a 'partial fusion of descent and locality ideology' " (Strathern 1979:95). This consideration of "actors' models and systems" (Kuper 1982b:88) as dynamic ideological constructs rather than fixed structures was taken back to Africa by researchers such as Karp (1978) and Van Leynseele (1979) and proved to be as relevant in an African context as in New Guinea. For Kuper the verdict was clear. He concluded that "the lineage model, its predecessors and its analogs, have no value for anthropological analysis" (1982b:92). With this curt epitaph Kuper dismissed the entire species of anthropology that had framed analyses of ancestor veneration in Africa up to that time. Clearly, Kuper's representation of the structural-functional position was somewhat caricatured particularly with regard to the works of Fortes and Evans-Pritchard (see Karp and Maynard 1983). Nevertheless, Kuper's article marked a broad waning of interest in kinship studies in Africa and a decline in research regarding ancestors.[2]

My field research convinces me ancestors continue to play an important role in the daily life of many people in West Africa. It is my intention to address the problem of ancestors from a new and I

think more productive perspective. While acknowledging the importance of ancestors in jural and political affairs, a theory of ancestors
must encompass a much broader scope of experience. I contend that
to understand the meaning of ancestors we must discard the boundaries of "cult" and "religion," which have traditionally defined the
field of inquiry. Instead, I will examine the experiential dimensions
of living in a social milieu that includes ancestors and the relationship of this experience to the construction and reproduction of historical consciousness and identity. By doing so, I hope to demonstrate the extent to which ancestor-related practices are techniques
for experientially engaging with the socially constituted past thus
providing cultural mechanisms with which people can make and
remake their social world. In this I am in agreement with Anthony
Giddens (1976, 1979) that the social world is not a given fact, external and coercive as in Durkheim's (1938) formulation, but rather is
continually constituted and reconstituted through the interrelations
of individuals engaged in the work of social praxis.

In Ohafia, notions of ethnicity, community, paternal and maternal descent groups—the components of every individual's sense of
himself or herself in relation to a multiplicity of social identities—
are products of knowledge of the past. This knowledge is grounded
in the lived experience of daily life in Ohafia villages and the fundamental conceptions of personhood that emerge from this experience. The categories of "who I am" and "who we are" are always
known in relation to "those who brought us into the world."

My exploration of ancestors necessarily begins at the locus of my
own research in Ohafia. However, my findings have much broader
implications pertaining to the general question of the role of ancestors in the cultures of sub-Saharan Africa. As I became established in
the rural farming communities of Ohafia and involved in the daily
flux of life, I came to appreciate the pervasiveness of the ancestral
presence in the lives of the people. The first problem that became
apparent was the complexity of the notion of ancestor. I found that
ancestors do not occupy a single "position" in a structural sense
but are embodied in a number of different ways in a wide range of
activities and material culture. These multiple manifestations suggested a variety of possible identities for ancestors rather than a uni-

fied model. It was this multivalent pervasiveness, and the particular way that Ohafia people engaged with the socially constructed experience of it, that constituted an *ancestral presence* in Ohafia life;[3] a presence that, immanent in the landscape itself, was attested to by the shrines found at every turn and the offerings of kola and palm wine that punctuated the daily flow of life.

## The Landscape of Names

Children begin to acquire knowledge of the ancestral presence when they accompany and assist their parents in work and social interaction. They travel to the farm, to market, and to the compounds of friends and relatives. They are sent running on errands to deliver yams, to fetch water, to bid a neighbor to visit, to perform countless tasks assisting in the progress of daily life and sociality. Through this participation in quotidian existence, they gain an emerging sense of the cultural environment. They discover the *names* of *places* and in doing so they learn that residential compounds are known by reference to the men who originally cleared the bush and established the site as cultural space. They learn that access to the constantly shifting mosaic of agricultural plots that demand their labor and provide their food is reckoned by reference to the names of ancestral mothers who farmed those plots ages ago.

This sense of inhabited and embodied history that informs the ancestral presence is not a formal abstraction transmitted by didactic procedures. It is a lived reality that develops over time through everyday experience. As the child navigates this terrain, tending to the small responsibilities assigned to him or her, this landscape of names begins to take shape: names of the dead, those people who cleared the land, built the compounds, farmed the land, and conceived the people. It is impossible to identify a particular place in the village without making reference to these names. They are simultaneously its history and its topography.

Residence in Ohafia is patrilocal, and compounds are composed of large houses occupied by senior males, surrounded by lines of smaller huts housing other family members. Typically, men's huts line one side of a path while women's huts line the other. The overall pattern is one of compact rows of contiguous structures traversed by a maze of paths. Amid this labyrinth of domestic space are numerous shrines, some hidden, some out in the open. One type, marked by a thin *oko* tree[4] surrounded by stones, is found in a small clearing near the patriarch's house. The tree marks the shrine as *ezi ra ali,* the place where mothers of that compound bring their new-born children to be blessed. The rite is a simple one performed by the eldest daughter of the paternal group. Rubbing the baby with chalk, she recites a brief blessing and places the child upon the ground. Until this rite is performed, mothers carefully avoid letting their infants touch the earth. The umbilical cord of each baby born to the compound is buried beneath the stones of the shrine.

Simple as it is, this rite embodies a fundamental relationship between individual, family, and land that is the crux of personhood in Ohafia. To question whether someone was ever placed on ezi ra ali is among the gravest of insults. Such a remark suggests that the person has no home, no family, that they are, in effect, not a person at all. Ezi ra ali means "compound and land." In this context "compound" refers to much more than a cluster of buildings. It is the physical manifestation of the paternal group in space and time, a history of occupation in which a place comes to represent the people, past and present, who have occupied it. The rite of ezi ra ali is an enactment of this identification between person, paternal descent, and place. It is a rite of *placement,* positioning each new child within a terrain, at once social, spatial, and temporal. As children grow older and come to know this terrain they find that it is etched with its own history that is their history as well. In the paternal compound in Ohafia, where generations have resided in the same place for centuries, the successive lives of those inhabitants, whose collective existence anthropologists attempt to capture in the notion of "patrilineage," are not only inscribed upon, but are constitutive of, the habitat itself. Naming practices also reflect the sense in which each person is understood, at a fundamental level, to be a living manifestation of the cumulative force of his paternal descent. Men's and women's names consist of their given names followed by their father's name and then their grandfather's name. This is usually the extent to which a name is given for social or legal purposes. But a person's *full* name is understood to go on and on, from father to father ad infinitum.[5]

The residential compounds are called *umudi*, "children of the same husband."[6] And these are known by the name of their common paternal ancestor. For instance, the people of the compound Ndi Kalu, literally, "people of Kalu," share a common ancestor named Kalu.[7] Among the buildings of this compound you will find the houses of Kalu's descendants. Beneath the floors of these houses the men who originally built them are buried. And the sons of the compound use the room over the grave as a meeting place where matters of family interest are discussed. When libations are poured the ancestors invoked are the founder of the compound in which the gathering takes place and his descendants. Before any living man may drink, a portion is poured into a small hole in the floor that is said to lead to the mouth of the founder himself.

Women are buried under the floor of their kitchen hut, which is located in the compound of their husband's family. Unlike men, who either build onto their father's compound, move into abandoned quarters, or found a new "extension" nearby, women are dislocated from their natal family after marriage. Women's existence in domestic space of the compound is transitory, and when a woman is buried beneath her kitchen it is often necessary to push aside the anonymous bones of other mothers who have passed before.

The system of double-unilineal descent practiced in Ohafia is spatialized in a binary system of land tenure. It is the patrilineage that dominates control of domestic property and activities and the matrilineage that controls access to farmlands. Hence, just as the names of male ancestors mark the social contours of the village terrain, so the names of female ancestors constitute points of reference for the distribution of the means of agricultural production.

Ancestresses are memorialized with pots called *ududu* that are kept embedded in the kitchen hearth of the eldest woman in the maternal descent group. This woman is priestess of the ududu and feeds them with yam and palm wine at the various points of the year, such as planting and harvest. When she performs these sacrifices—placing small amounts of food in the pots and sprinkling them with wine—she entreats the ancestral mothers to assure the well-being of their descendants. The priestess of the ududu knows the pots and calls each by name when she offers sacrifice. She is the official genealogist of the maternal descent group, and she is always consulted if disagreement arises over descent as it bears upon rights to productive land. Thus, both the spiritual and mundane functions of this shrine relate directly to agriculture, assuring the bountiful production and proper distribution of agricultural land, respectively. The ududu reside at the core of female space: the hearth of the priestess of the maternal descent group. Each time a priestess dies and is succeeded, the shrine must shift its location to the hearth of the new priestess, usually in some other compound and often in another village.

Male ancestors are also memorialized with pots that are called *ifu mọṅ* meaning "spirit face."[8] Unlike the ududu, the ifu mọṅ have a jural role. Oaths taken on the ifu mọṅ are used to settle disputes, and it is said that any false statement sworn at the face of one's ancestors will bring death to the speaker. The ifu mọṅ also serve as a reminder of Ohafia's martial past. These are the shrines of great warriors of the precolonial age, and trophy skulls are displayed near the pots as a vivid reminder of prowess of the ancestral fathers. The ifu mọṅ are located in small structures set aside for that purpose and that of the senior patrilineage is situated in or around the meetinghouse (*obu*) used by the male elders. The groupings of paternal compounds around a common meetinghouse are known as *ọnụ ogo,* and they carry the names of ancestors even more remote in history. The term *ogo* refers to the open commons around which the individual compounds are grouped. The term *ọnụ* means "mouth" or "doorway." Hence, *ọnụ ogo* refers to the fact that this mid-ranking structure of village organization stands on the threshold between the domestic space of the umudi and the public space of the ogo.

Ọnụ ogo are grouped into larger divisions called *isi ogo* or "head ogo." These are traced to the original founders of the village who are often represented by statuary in or around the ogo. Large villages may have as many as four of these isi ogo.[9] The term *ogo* refers to the open commons itself and, by metonymic extension, to the grouping of compounds that share the commons. In its broadest application

Fig. 7.   Ifu mọṅ (literally, "ancestral spirit face") receives a
sacrifice in honor of patrilineal ancestors. *(Akanu Ohafia
1990)*

the term *ogo* means village. The ogo is a public space where people
meet and where dances and masquerade performances take place. It
is the site at which expressive representations of kindred community
and shared past are situated.

Every performance in an ogo is positioned in space by a oratory
that serves as a performative evocation of the ancestral history. Such
events begin with a call and response that emphasizes consensus. The
orator calls the name of the ogo followed by the entreaty, *kwenụ!*
which is a call to respond to the orator's pronouncement. To this the
gathered crowd replies with an affirmative *"hụ!"* Then the village
section is called by name to agree and again the reply: *"hụ!"* The village is called by name, then Ohafia as a whole, and each time solidar-
ity is signaled by a resounding *"hụ!"* This oratorical device that introduces nearly every public statement or performance is an elegant
expression of the concentric levels of inclusion that constitute Ohafia
social identity. At major events the sweep of identity is extended to
include Igbo, Nigeria, and on occasion Africa. At most public events

this introduction is followed by an offering of libations for ancestors. As the orator pours wine or gin on the ground the founder of the ogo and his successors are called to come and share the wine and join in the festivities. These ancestors are asked to bless their descendants with good fortune and health. In this way the names of ancestors associated with the place of performance are ceremonially linked to the unfolding situation and the ambitions of those gathered in that space. These libations recall common ancestry to the collective memory and evoke in Ohafia people an experiential realization of their shared links of place and family.

The representation of kindred community elicited in public oration and physically embodied in the landscape of names suggests a vast kinship chart. It is an indigenous model of segmentary society in which each level of inclusion and exclusion is elicited in performance and inscribed upon the terrain by monuments to common ancestry. This indigenous Ohafia representation of social time and space is analogous in structure to the anthropological models of kinship proposed by Evans-Pritchard and Fortes. However, as critics have observed, this indigenous model is an idiom of identity rather than a charting of patterns of descent. In practice, the landscape of names is a dynamic lived phenomenon, and it is continually molded and reshaped. Unlike a fixed map, it is made up of multiple representations of the past that may interact to produce many potential forms, many possible interpretations. Ohafia's history is continually constituted and reconstituted. It is a knowledge of the past that lives in the experience of the village inhabitants themselves: agents of the selective memory of history.

## Loci of Knowledge, Truth, and Power

The "official" past expressed in the naming of compounds and continually reproduced in oratory is a history of inclusion and common descent. In this representation, the historical processes by which the community has been constructed are submerged in an overwhelming sense of commonality and kinship. However, if we return to the contours of the experiential landscape we find that detailed knowledges of these histories are associated with shrines known as *arụnsi* that are found near the boundaries of paternal compounds, at the edge of the bush, and in springs. The narratives associated with arụnsi contain knowledge of migrations, social disruptions, and other discontinuities of the past. Scrupulously preserved, these potentially polarizing knowledges often come to light in times of crisis and social negotiation. The priests of these shrines harbor stories of the men who established the shrines to "cool the land" and make it habitable. Unlike the official oratorical references to the ancestral founders, these are nonvalorized tales of homeless men, often outcasts, who were forced to establish new homes.

Most of these stories recall the age prior to the twentieth century. At that time the men of Ohafia and other neighboring groups were warriors who often participated in martial expositions organized by the chiefs in Arochukwu to the south of Ohafia. The Aro built an empire on the land, slaves, and booty acquired through these internecine battles. The Ohafia, however, received few of these rewards. Their primary interest was the acquisition of human trophy heads. These heads were highly coveted because young men were required by their age-grades to bring heads from battle as proof of manhood. Men who had taken many heads in battle were regarded as "heroes" and enjoyed much influence in their villages. An elaborate and somewhat unstable network of peace treaties and contracts prevented the men of these communities from taking the heads of people residing in the regional groups. These included not only the villages of Ohafia and Arochukwu, but also the neighboring villages in Abam to the east, Abiriba to the northeast, and Nkporo to the northwest. Ohafia men would tell me that the Ohafia man of that period maintained two faces. The outward-looking face—that which regarded the outside world—was that of a ruthless warrior whose desire for heads was paramount. The inward-looking face—that which regarded his own domain of regional and domestic affairs— was that of a negotiator, peacemaker, husband, and father. These two paradoxical ideals of manhood were played out in many of the stories of Ohafia's past associated with arụnsi. The following story was abridged from one told to me by an arụnsi priest of Ndi Awa compound in Akanu, Ohafia.

The father of this compound was called Udumali. He was living at Nkporo and had a compatriot named Odaukwu who lived at Abiriba. The two of them were brave men who traveled here and there to cut human heads. There were times that both of them took the heads of Abiriba people. When this was discovered they were driven out of these communities so they moved into Ohafia, Udumali at Amaekpu and Odaukwu at Elu. While there, Udumali gave birth to a son whom he named Awa Imaga, after the person with whom he lived in Amaekpu. The two men continued their head collecting and were soon driven from these villages and moved down to Ububa. But they had trouble in Ububa, and Odaukwu's wife advised her husband and Udumali to leave that place and go to the home of her family at Amuke. They moved to Amuke but soon a dispute arose between the two men. One day they went hunting and killed seven animals. In the sharing, Odaukwu claimed that he would take the heads. Udumali also claimed the right to the heads [claiming the heads is a right of seniority, which in the case of two men who became established in the village at the same time is ambiguous]. Udumali, knowing that they had come there together, decided that he could not live under Odaukwu so he performed a ritual separation. He coiled a leaf into a cone and filled it with soup which he drank saying "two fish will not be put together on a single stick" (a single compound cannot contain the two men). Udumali moved to what is now Isi Ugwu. He sent his second son, Awa Imaga, to live in nearby Akanu. Before Awa Imaga left he went to a stream in Isi Ugwu called Iyinta at which there was an arụnsi. The arụnsi asked him to bring it out of the earth and through the water. He did this, and the arụnsi was brought here to protect the new compound of Awa in Akanu. The arụnsi is called Nkuma Ndi Awa (stone of the descendants of Awa). To this day, the sons of this compound go to that stream in Isi Ugwu each year at planting time to offer sacrifice.

This story revolves around motifs of criminality, exile, conflict, and homelessness. The tension between the value that Ohafia culture traditionally put on violent bravery and the potentially disruptive consequences of such violence is central. That these two head-strong men were finally able to settle their differences through a ritual act of truce (drinking from the leaf) rather than killing one another barely balances (and certainly doesn't "mediate") this anti-social representation of a founding father.

A "founder" is often a person without a home and in need of one: a person "out of place," to paraphrase Mary Douglas. Kopytoff (1987:18) has observed that "African societies were so constructed that they systematically produced frontiersmen" and he cites the common theme in African history of the migration of "the disgruntled, the victimized, the exiled, the refugees, the losers in internecine struggles, the adventurous, and the ambitious."

That this ragged lot are the source of that most exalted category of ancestor—the "founding father"—would seem to contradict the common observation that only those who have lived long and morally upright lives can attain the status of ancestorhood (see Uchendu 1976:293). My inquiries revealed that—as the preceding story demonstrates—it is often scandal, conflict, or disaster that leads to a particular individual attaining the status of "founding father." This is not merely a product of the disjuncture between the present day and a past removed to quasi-mythical times. It is an ongoing process that can be witnessed in the present. The following is an abridged example from my own field notes.

> As I was walking from a remote compound back to the village with two friends, we left the main path to take a shortcut through a large maize field adjacent to the village. As we reached the crest of a hill we came across a fresh and unmarked grave. Knowing that this was a strange place for a grave, I asked what circumstances had led to a burial in this unlikely spot. One of my companions explained that this man had lived most of his adult life in a distant city and had failed to return home periodically to share his wealth, maintain his links with his relations in the village, and retain a room in his compound. While men often pursue careers in distant locations it was vital that they return periodically to affirm their family ties and maintain a room in the compound. Membership in the paternal descent

group is marked by maintenance of a personal space in the paternal compound, and upon death a man should be buried under the floor of this room. Those who fail to maintain this symbolic presence are referred to as "lost sons." When this particular man's body was returned to the village for burial there was no appropriate place to bury it, and so he was interred in a maize field. The entire situation was scandalous and constituted a great embarrassment for his family. As this explanation was completed my other companion suddenly chimed in: "but his son could correct the situation if he were to build a new compound over the grave." It took me a moment to recognize the significance of this remark. I asked: "Then what would that compound be called?" "It would be named after this man," he answered, pointing at the mound of earth.

Posterity is not concerned with whether the man is buried under the floor or the floor built over the grave. Socially constructed images of the past are complex, shifting, and multivocal. They manifest as representations of social/spatial relations as well as historical/temporal ones. The boundaries between the public knowledge of oration and the ritually obscured knowledge of the shrines are simultaneously social and topographic. This realization is essential to an understanding of the power manifest in the shrines themselves. Arunsi are arbiters of truth. Oaths taken on them are bound by death. They can be called upon to punish thieves and wrongdoers and are said to respond quickly and ruthlessly. While I was living in Ohafia, a woman was struck by lightning while she was violating the taboo prohibiting people from going to their farms when a family member has died. No one doubted that Kalu (an arunsi associated with lightning) had "met" her. The village landscape is punctuated with arunsi. They physically mark the passages between one kindred grouping and another and consecrate the shared space of the ogo. These shrines constitute loci of truth and power. Rituals and aesthetically framed performances employ such places, and the ritual objects associated with them, in strategic manipulations and reconstructions of the interstices of social relations. Thus, a multiplicity of histories permeates the village environment, each with the power to evoke a cluster of relations and identities rooted in the past.

One of the most vividly elaborated expressions of a history associated with an aṛunsi in Ohafia is the *Ọkwankọ* masquerade of the hamlet of Ndi Mba in the village of Ohafia. Performed each year during the New Yam festival, Ọkwankọ involves a full day of music and dance and a series of performances by sixteen masked figures. The masqueraders sing in the dialect of Abiriba, a group of villages to the northwest of Ohafia. Each mask is carried by a representative of one of the various paternal groupings said to be descended from the original founder who is believed to have migrated from Abiriba over two centuries ago. In this day-long performance the foreign origin of the compound, normally effaced by the unifying rhetoric of Ohafia clanship, is celebrated.

As with the earlier story of the aṛunsi of Ndi Awa where it was necessary to conduct a yearly pilgrimage to the site of origin to offer sacrifice, the yearly performance of Ọkwankọ "fills the space between Abiriba and Ohafia."[10] In contrast to the rhetoric of identity that usually prevails, the performance of Ọkwankọ is a celebration of alterity. It foregrounds the foreign origins of the residents of Ndi Mba in a dramatic presentation of masks that are distinct in style and form from any of the masks common to Ohafia communities. When I investigated Ọkwankọ it was emphasized that the masks did not represent *ndichin* (ancestors) or *mọṅ* (ancestral spirits) but that they were aṛunsi. Aṛunsi embody and focus the tremendous power that is associated with truth and with alterity. In the case of Ọkwankọ this includes the power to heal illness and cure barrenness in women. As a result the women of Ndi Mba are said to be free of barrenness but other people can also approach the elders of the compound and request treatment by the aṛunsi. The connection between aṛunsi and ancestors is not one of direct identity, and the power of aṛunsi should not be construed as something that is attributed to ancestral spirits. However, as bearers of truth, aṛunsi act as historical markers that place ancestors in a historical landscape. These shrines, masks, stones, and streams are loci of power that resolve discontinuity and difference even as they celebrate it. They faithfully record the disjunctures of history that have recently come to dominate discussions of African social organization. But the truths of aṛụnsi are not heard as voices in opposition to the rhetoric of kindred community but rather as another level of complexity. The ifu mọṅ of paternal ancestors that stand as markers of shared kinship are also considered to function as aṛụnsi particularly to the extent that they are sites where oaths can be taken and absolute truth established. They serve as markers of shared kinship and also as the locus of histories that record the historical disruptions of the past. Thus they exist simultaneously as symbols of identity and symbols of alterity.


## Rethinking Heuristically

In summary, the structural-functional model of ancestor "cults" as a component in a system of jural authority and land tenure appeared to reach a dead end when the theories of lineage and segmentary social organization upon which this hypothesis depended were called into question. Ethnographic and historical research indicated a preponderance of migratory activities and a high degree of discontinuity and reorganization in kin relations. Thus it was concluded that the models of traditional African social organization proposed by Evans-Pritchard and Fortes were too static to be compatible with the dynamism evident in African historical processes. I have suggested that the structural-functional model of ancestor-related practices reached its epitome in Kopytoff's (1971) article "Ancestors as Elders in Africa." I have also noted that the historical model of African social dynamics was cogently formulated by Kopytoff (1987) sixteen years later in his introduction to *The African Frontier*. On the basis of my own data I suggest that both the structural-functional model of social stasis and the historical model of social dynamics are parallel to indigenous modes of knowledge such as those embodied in the representations of the past found in Ohafia. In academic discourse these two models might seem to be opposed. They are taken to constitute "schools of thought" that provide incompatible explanatory arguments. However, both of these representations form an aspect of the Ohafia people's lived experience of truth. Unlike academic discourse, which tends toward reduction of experience to noncontradictory, essentialized, and universalized truths, lived experience encompasses, indeed even demands, multiple truths. In his essay "On Ethnographic Truth" Michael Jackson (1989:187) concludes with the possibility that "truth is not binding. It is in the interstices as much as it is in the structure, in fiction as much as in fact."

What may appear to be contradictory in theoretical abstraction becomes, in the richness of lived experience, part of a complex whole. This insight is essential if we are to avoid positivistic tendencies toward reductionism. A truly nonreductionistic approach to ancestors in Africa must account for the fact that while previous theories do not contain *the* truth they do reveal glimpsed truths. In Ohafia, differing representations of the past act as complementary bodies of knowledge, with their own domains of application. Could it be that the scientific quest for the best explanation is more a product of our rhetorical practices than it is an "objective" process for the construction of a scientific truth? I suggest that Ohafia's multifaceted view of social dynamics in time and space allows for the possibility that seemingly contradictory "paradigms" simply reflect different perspectives and that privileging one or the other for the sake of argument diminishes our understanding of the whole. The Ohafia model of knowledge (and I suspect many others) represents truth as an irreducible, multifaceted object. In Ohafia, the embodied spirit that is manifest in masquerade performance is an enactment of the play of truth and illusion through which all human knowledge exists. The fact that it is a man in a costume in no way diminishes the truth that it is an embodied spirit. In remarking on the irreducible quality of this knowledge, proverbial wisdom advises that "you cannot watch a masquerade from only one position." Thus, in evaluating the knowledge that our anthropological ancestors have bestowed upon us it may be wise to remember the wisdom inherent in the Ohafia view: that truth can not be found in the valorization or vilification of our predecessors but in learning to thoughtfully retrace the paths that lead to where we are today.

# PART 3

# Beyond Tradition and Modernity

Power must be analyzed as something which circulates, or rather as something which only functions in the form of a chain. It is never located here or there, never in anyone's hands, never appropriated as a commodity or piece of wealth.

(Foucault 1980:98)

Ike dị na awaja na awaja. (Power runs in many channels.)
Igbo proverb, translated by Chinua Achebe

(Cole and Aniakor 1984:ix)

CHAPTER 6

# Portrait of a Brave Woman

$W$hen Nne Uko Uma Awa was asked why she was known to dress like a man, she responded:

> Yes, I like that question! I dressed like a man because by creation I was meant to be a man. But as it happened, when coming into this world I came with a woman's body. That is why I dressed that way. (Awa 1991b: 19-A-02)

This is the story of Nne Uko Uma Awa, a woman of the village of Akanu. In the course of Nne Uko's life she often dressed in men's clothes. But this was the least of her distinguishing characteristics. Nne Uko married two wives, joined various men's societies including the celebrated Ekpe (leopard) society, and gained the right to dance with men when they performed the Ohafia warrior's dance. While female husbands are relatively common among the patrilineal Igbo (Talbot 1932:195–96; Uchendu 1965:7), they are rare among the Ohafia Igbo where agricultural land is largely held by maternal descent groups. Nne Uko is known in her community as a *dike nwami*—a term that in Ohafia is variously translated as "heroine," "warrior woman," and, most frequently, "brave woman."

I will begin with a discussion of the traditions associated with dike nwami in Ohafia and then present further excerpts from my interview with Nne Uko, including exegesis as necessary. I suggest that the common assumptions of Ohafia people regarding dike nwami and Nne Uko's interpretation of her own life add provocative new voices to the anthropological literature on female husbands. Nne Uko's story, however, does more than enhance our understanding of woman-to-woman marriage. Her reflections on her own life can be read as a heuristic guide pointing toward a richer understanding of the play of individual, society, and contingent events in the constitution of social praxis.


## Legendary Warrior Women

The ancestors of the Ohafia people were renowned as mighty and ruthless warriors. In precolonial times Ohafia men were not considered to have attained full status as adult males until they returned from war with a human head as a battle trophy. While the era of internecine warfare is now over, the stories of the great warriors of Ohafia are recorded in the songs of the war dance. The heroes of these epics provide idealized images of masculine courage and accomplishment. Many of the epic songs, however, also include accounts of women. Some of these women are "the great mothers" (Azuonye 1974:510). War dance singers recount the story of one such mother, Ugoenyi, who loses two sons in battle. Fearing for her third son, she dresses him as a girl so that he will not be taken to war with his age-mates. His peers, however, discover the masquerade and take him by force. When he returns victorious with a trophy head, his mother's joy is such that she raises a great celebration in his honor for which a special music and dance are created. This, it is said, is the origin of the war dance (Azuonye 1974:490–94).

This motif of brave deeds as catalyst for a transformation from feminine to masculine is also associated with another, more extraordinary type of woman prevalent in some of the epics. These women adopt the characteristics of warriors themselves. They are *dike nwami,* brave woman who go to the battlefield, risk their lives, and take trophy heads like their male counterparts. Structurally parallel to the heroic return of Ugoenyi's son, their transmutation of gendered behavior and their heroic actions transform tragedy into celebration. Such exceptional characters and circumstances are often central to myth and legend. An initial setting in which the normal order of things is skewed or reversed often constitutes the project of the narrative itself: a resolution of order. This is certainly the case in the story of Ugoenyi's son. By taking a head in battle, he puts things right by doing what is appropriate for an Ohafia man to do. He becomes a man by acting like a man. These warrior heroes embody traditional values with which men identify and refer directly to their own sense of themselves as Ohafia men. Head-taking, reprehensible in the present-day context, is dissociated from its actual practice and is reconstituted in performance as an icon of masculine attainment. For men, achievements considered to be equivalent to head-taking condense a diverse cluster of values such as personal accomplishment, courage, and the incorporation of power. The legendary heroines present a more difficult problem. In Ohafia, motherhood is considered to be the definitive marker of womanhood. The dike nwami, however, achieve recognition through heroic acts.

For instance, the epic of Inyan Olugu, as recorded by Azuonye, recounted the story of a young woman whose husband had not taken a head in battle. She vowed that she would take a head herself and give the honor to her husband. She went with her husband to Nkalu, a place where the people spoke "neither Igbo nor in stammer." Upon arrival, she sent her husband up a palm tree to pick fruits for her. While he was there, five Nkalu men approached. Inyan Olugu took her husband's gun and killed all five, cutting off their heads, which she put in a "long basket."[1] She told her husband of her accomplishment, and when they returned to their village she took the heads to the great *ikoro,* the massive slit drum where trophy heads were traditionally honored. The warriors of the village came to sing the praises of her husband, but she told them to sing not only his praises, but also the praises of Inyan Olugu: "she that kills and packs in a long basket, the woman who won heads and gave the honor to her husband" (Azuonye 1974:405–8).

Likewise, the epic of Nne Mgbafo tells the story of a woman who, when her husband didn't return from battle, dressed herself like a warrior and went to Ibibioland in search of him. She found her way to the scene of the battle and searched among the heaps of headless corpses for the body of her husband. Accounts of her adventure vary. In one version she found her husband's body, buried it, sacrificed a goat, and then later captured a man and sacrificed him on the grave as well. In other variants she found he had been taken prisoner and intimidated his captors so aggressively that they released him to her. In another version she found her husband alive but learned that he had taken no head in battle and so, like Inyan Olugu, she decapitated a man herself and gave the head to her husband as his own trophy (Azuonye 1983:348–68). In each case she returned home triumphant and was celebrated by her community as a dike nwami (1983:348–68; 1990:68–69).

These stories of women who fulfill the Ohafia ordeal of manhood in spite of their sex seem to celebrate an overthrow of cultural norms rather than providing a resolution. These women do what men should have done but failed to do. The legends memorialize anomalous women driven by circumstances to defy the limits of the feminine role. The relationship between legends of Ohafia heroism and the construction of male identity in everyday life is explicitly drawn by Ohafia people when the war dance is performed for successful men. However, the question remains: how do these "brave women" of legend, also generalized cultural archetypes, relate to the particular life experiences of women in Ohafia? Like the dike nwami of old, the people of Akanu stressed that Nne Uko was an exceptional woman—one distinguished from others by her heroic actions.

## A Living Legend

When I went to Nne Uko's compound I brought cooked meat, fish, and a bottle of gin, as is customary when visiting a prominent elder. My arrival attracted much attention in the compound. Though I had made prior arrangements for the interview I had to explain my visit to a large group of Nne Uko's kinspeople. Many insisted that they should be included in the meeting (and the feasting). One of her brothers argued that his presence was essential if we were to get the whole story. The negotiations were adeptly managed by my friend and research collaborator Ibe Nwosu Kalu. Throughout these preliminaries Nne Uko remained, in chiefly fashion, in her hut. At length I approached her home accompanied by a large entourage. It was ostensibly a typical Ohafia female abode, a bedroom and kitchen divided by a partition. But the new metal roof and wooden shutters contrasted with the thatched structures around it, indicating that she was person of means.

Nne Uko greeted us with a broad smile. She was an elderly woman, probably in her late seventies or early eighties.[2] She was dressed in elegant women's clothing: a white blouse with eyelet lace at the neck and an imported wrap skirt embroidered with metallic thread. Her unwrapped head revealed a crown of hair as white as chalk. Despite her advanced age, her eyes were bright and attentive. Her features possessed a fineness that could not be obscured by her many years. Perhaps sharing my thoughts Ink whispered to me, "She was a beautiful woman in her time." As we waited for the others to assemble I observed objects of particular significance in the room—things that were not usually found in a woman's hut. On one wall hung an *akparanja,* the traditional cutlass of Ohafia warriors. Near it hung a *mma ji,* a yam knife, now practically obsolete as a tool, but still serving as a trophy indicating recognition as a great yam farmer.[3] Also prominent was a finely carved *ṅkpa,* or walking stick, decorated with velvet, an accessory normally carried by a "big man" of great achievement. When everyone was seated and had exchanged greetings, Nne Uko requested the gin. A young man produced a small shot glass and, filling it to the brim, handed it to her. With a steady hand she began tipping the glass slightly, sprinkling gin on the floor, and as she did this she accompanied the libation with these words:

Father Uma Awa Ogba,
Father Digbo Odo,
Kalu Uma Awa,
Awa Uma Awa, here is wine.
Agwu Uma Awa, here is wine.
Mong Ogba, here is wine.
Father Uma Awa Odo, here is wine.
Ukariwe Uma Awa, here is wine.
It is me Uko Uma Awa.
It was you who prepared me to act.
I am not acting on my own power.
It is by the power you have given me that I act.

My father and mother raised me to live as they lived.
John, man of America,
Man of Utugokoko,
Man of my town,
He has come today, Orie Ohafia Uduma Ezema.
Today is Orie, the day my father used to farm yams.
He has come to know Uko Uma Awa.
May things go well him in the morning,
And may they go well in the evening.
Father, may things go well with his son who was once here.
May things go well with his wife and with his baby.
Chineke, Ọbasị above,
Life for the great person,
Life for the small person.[4]

(Awa 1991a:19-A-01)

With these formalities complete Nne Uko began to explain to us her belief that she was "meant to be a man." Curious to find the source of this conviction Ink asked, "Was there anything that made you decide that you should act as a man? Because in your childhood you were seen to be very agile and strong and very manly in behavior." Nne Uko replied:

One's interests are apparent in childhood. I was interested in manly activities. I can not tell where this came from, this understanding that I was meant to be a man. But I took up manly activities because I was drawn to them. In those days, when a maiden came to the age of marriage she stayed in the fattening house for three years.[5] At this time I completed all the maiden rites including *igbu ewu* [literally, "to kill a goat"]. It is one of the ceremonies that must be done before a woman is wedded. . . . I completed all the requirements of maidenhood until I reached womanhood. After attaining womanhood I went as my nature was given to me—to behave as a man. (Awa 1991b:19-A-02)

Even in her participation in the girls' coming-of-age ceremonies Nne Uko distinguished herself as one who excelled in manly accomplishments. Accounts of the events surrounding Nne Uko's coming-of-age ceremonies came to me from various sources. An elderly ritual specialist named Kalu Omiko told me that in those days, when the rites for girls were performed, a group of boys who were their age-mates were required to go on a ritual hunt and catch a species of small antelope known as *aṅwụ*.[6] They had to capture the creature by hand so it could be brought back alive and sacrificed at the shrine of Kalu Akanu (Kamalu), the force identified with thunder and lightning, which was the tutelary deity of the village of Akanu. But in the year of Nne Uko's coming-of-age, something happened that transformed the character of the ceremony. That year, a woman in the compound that held the priesthood of Kalu Akanu had a prophetic dream. In this dream Kalu came to her and demanded that on this occasion the sacrifice must be captured by the girls of the age-set rather than the boys. Dreams are the channel normally used by spirits to demand sacrifice, and women are often the receptors of such requests.[7] It could not be ignored. So that year, against all precedent, the ritual hunt was conducted by girls. For Nne Uko, who had always joined the young boys in competitions and hunting games, this divine intervention was taken as a personal challenge and an opportunity to excel. Nne Uko recalled:

> The *arụnsi,* Kalu Akanu demanded a sacrifice. And the sacrifice required was an animal called *aṅwụ* which the young women had to catch by hand. This was a fast animal but we had to catch it. I was the leader of the hunt. . . . When we went I dressed in an *ọnụgwe* [warrior's loin cloth] and an *okpu agụ* [warrior's "leopard" hat]. I tied on an akparanja [warrior's cutlass] in a sheath. . . . I was the leader dressed as a warrior man. . . . Then we went down to the village, marched around the village and finally hung the *aṅwụ* on Kalu Akanu. After that I often dressed in that way. (Awa 1991b:19-A-02)

It was on this occasion that Nne Uko first became known among the villagers as a *dike nwami*—a brave woman—the same term used to refer to the warrior women of legend. By dressing as a warrior for the ritual hunt, Nne Uko employed bodily presentation and the symbolic potential of clothing to link herself with the Ohafia warrior legacy. By acting as a warrior she boldly seized upon the most powerful and exclusive markers of Ohafia heroism as celebrated in the Ohafia war dance.

Regarding Nne Uko's participation in the war dance, Ink later commented, "Women are allowed to dance iri agha [the war dance] but they have their style. Nne Uko, being what she is, used to dance as [a] man, . . . performing *ofufu* as men do" (Kalu 1992).

Having completed the maiden's rites, Nne Uko married but time passed and she did not conceive a child. During the interview Nne Uko never mentioned this, but other people's accounts of her life emphasized her "failure to conceive" (Kalu 1991c:16-A-00; Omiko 1991:30-B-01; Ojiono 1991:23-A-01). In Africa, childlessness is nearly always represented as a misfortune, and this rhetoric may mask those occasions when women choose not to have children. In the West we tend to translate this representation in medical terms, interpreting this representation of the childless condition as "barrenness" or "infertility." In fact, it is often perceived as a condition of ill fate rather than dysfunctional physiology, and appeals to ancestors and fertility spirits are appropriate treatments. It is impossible to really know whether Nne Uko was infertile or whether she intentionally avoided becoming pregnant.[8] In any case, childlessness helped her to cultivate and maintain her status as a brave woman. In Ohafia it was not unusual for marriages to dissolve when they did not produce children, and this was the case with Nne Uko's union. However, she was already known as a dike nwami and she began to make her way in the community by means normally reserved for men.

In Ohafia, farming rights were inherited primarily through the maternal descent group, and the allocation of farmlands was usually determined by the elder men of the maternal descent group. Nne Uko, as a young woman, would normally have only had access to marginal lands, but her status as a dike nwami entitled her to special consideration. She exhibited great skill at farming, secured good land, and began to accumulate wealth. When she was financially able, she traveled to Ibibio country and acquired a wife. Over time she took another wife in this fashion. Seeking wives from families external to Ohafia was necessary in order to avoid a contradiction in the matrilineal system of inheritance in Ohafia. As a woman, Nne Uko's children would be members of her matrilineage, and they would inherit the right to farm the land she had farmed. If she had taken Ohafia wives, her children would have belonged to two different matrilineages, an impossible absurdity because it would imply they were born of two different mothers.[9] In his brief study of Ohafia customs, Uche (1960:46) discusses the means for restoring lineage continuity by "adoptive" marriage.

> The [Ohafia] people dislike childlessness since this implies that the family shrine [*ududu*] will in course of time become neglected. In most serious cases when a family is fast dying out, then the course open to its surviving members is to extend the boundaries of the family by adoption through marriage.

By "adoption through marriage" Uche refers to the practice of adopting non-Ohafia women into the maternal descent group by way of their marriage to male (or in cases such as Nne Uko's, female) members of the group. As Nne Uko told me about her wives, she laughed and said: "Now you will want to know if I took them to bed!" She maintained she had not.[10] Her wives had children (with assistance from her brother), and with the help of her wives and her children she continued to distinguish herself as a farmer and to accumulate wealth.

It should be noted that the honorific *Nne* that was used by everyone who referred to Uko Uma Awa literally means "mother." It is a term of respect accorded to women with adult children. The role of Nne Uko's brother, the biological father of "her" children, appeared to be ambiguous. Throughout the interview he maintained a slightly proprietary attitude toward her and occasionally interrupted to finish her answers to questions. When we got to the subject of Nne Uko's wives and their children, Ink asked about her relationship to the young man who had built her house. Her brother aggressively interrupted and asserted that he was the father of the builder. Later Nne Uko stated, "Those women I married have their children. These children are taking very good care of me as their mother and, in fact, as their father." Her brother interrupted at this point (in a transparent attempt to change the subject) to observe that Nne Uko was the first woman to wear canvas shoes while working on her farm, which had, up until then, been worn only by men.

In time her successful farming enabled her to take yam titles in ceremonies that gave recognition to farmers who amassed large stocks of yams and shared their wealth and food with the community. Ultimately her influence extended beyond the realm of farming, and she was able to gain initiation into various men's societies including the region's most exclusive men's organization, the Ekpe society. Unlike some men's societies in other West African communities, not all men become members of Ekpe. Only elite men (those who pass the social litmus test and can pay the high cost of the ceremony) are taught the meaning of the secret language of gesture and the hieroglyphs that cover the cloth wrappers worn by initiates. While the initiation of a woman into the Ekpe society is not unprecedented it is an extremely rare occurrence. Ekpe society is a men's organization, and members are sworn not to reveal the secrets to their wives. Ajike Kalu commented, "It is very rare for women to be initiated into Ekpe society, except the Calabar people." Talbot (1912:44) noted that elderly women (presumably postmenopause) were sometimes initiated into the lower ranks of Calabar Ekpe societies. Ekpe elders in Akanu could recall only one other instance of a female initiate in Ohafia: a woman from the village of Asaga who, like Nne Uko, was known as a dike nwami.[11] Of her membership in Ekpe, Nne Uko commented:

> During my youthful period, the Ekpe society danced in obu Ndi Odo which was very close to my residence. Then, considering my activities, my inclination to challenge men at the things they did, I was called up to be initiated into the Ekpe society. It was due to my activities and brave actions. . . . Lots of those societies that men belong to, I also belong to them. Many of the activities of men, I took part. (Awa 1991b:19-A-02)

Her brother then added:

In those days, as a strong woman, if a man offered a case of gin, she would offer a case of gin. If a man offered a goat, she would offer a goat. Showing that what men could do, she could do. She also had to initiate on behalf of other people. Even those that were from her father's side. (Awa 1991b:19-A-02)

Ajike then noted that, in addition to her role in men's societies, Nne Uko had been a leader of women when they mobilized to protest the actions of the men of the community. "She is one of those who lead such missions. These are some of the things that lead us to call her a brave woman." Asked to comment, Nne Uko explained:

At times, when the men put restrictions on women, made decisions which were against us. We, the women, would refuse adhering to the decision and we refused to go to anywhere [to work on the farms and in the market]. We would stay at home and sort it out with the men. (Awa 1991b:19-A-02)

I asked if she could recollect a specific instance of such a "women's strike."

Yes, there was an instance when there was a quarrel between men and women and things which were not supposed to be said about women were said. The women were so offended that all the women in the village left and traveled to Ebem [a neighboring village]. The men knew that they could not remain in Akanu without their wives. They had to go down and appeal to the women to come back. Which at last they did. . . . When such an exodus takes place then the men must send a representative to the clan head of the village where the women have gone and appeal to him with a bottle of wine, a goat, and other things. They must ask the chief to appeal to their women to join them and go back to their village. . . . I was involved in that women's exodus to Ebem. (Awa 1991b:19-A-02)

I asked Nne Uko when this had occurred. She chuckled and said, "A child of those days has become a grandmother by now."

In the course of Nne Uko's life, she established herself as a community leader and did so by proving herself as a leader among women as well as utilizing means that were usually accessible only to men. Now, in her old age, the trappings of manly achievement hung on her walls as memorials to her exceptional life. She no longer participated in Ekpe activities or other masculine pursuits. Instead she adopted the life-style associated with prominent elder females. The children of her wives referred to her as "grandmother." She was taken care of by her children and had risen to a position as priestess of her matrilineage's *ududu* shrine, offering sacrifice to the ancestresses in her maternal line.

The ududu shrine consists of pots kept on the hearth of the matriarch of the maternal descent group. Each pot represents an ancestress and each is given yam and palm wine by the priestess during various agricultural rites. These pots serve as markers of the genealogy of the maternal group. The priestess knows each by name and she is consulted when disputes arise regarding descent group history and land rights. As priestess of the ududu shrine Nne Uko is regarded as the current matriarch of her matrilineage, and when she dies, she will have an ududu pot raised to her by her successor. She will be remembered, honored, and receive sacrifices as an ancestress to her maternal descent group. Those who claim descent from Nne Uko will farm the lands she once farmed: lands significantly expanded in her celebrated career.

This account of a woman who, in spite of childlessness, managed to position herself to become an ancestress to her matrilineage raises a number of questions about the relationship of human agency to the constitution of social roles. When I originally heard about Nne Uko I imagined she had "become a man." After hearing her own story it became clear she never abandoned womanhood. Rather, she was known as a particular kind of woman: a dike nwami. Throughout her life Nne Uko was recognized in her community as a woman, socially and otherwise. Ultimately she attained a privileged office of female authority. Nne Uko's claim, however, that she was "supposed to be a man" introduced an additional concept of gendered personhood that, while independent of apparent physiological characteristics, was represented in her narrative as a disposition present and expressed long before gender recoding might have been necessitated by social concerns arising from her childlessness.

## Determinism or Destiny?

Nne Uko established herself as a dike nwami before she was married. Her unique disposition for "manly" achievements was socially recognized before anyone conceived of her as a "barren" woman. This fact is at the heart of Nne Uko's explanation of her life: her conviction that she "was supposed to be a man." On the surface Nne Uko would seem to be what O'Brien (1977:113) called an "autonomous female husband": a barren woman who was able to maintain her social status by taking wives and claiming their children as her descendants. But for such a categorization to serve explanatory ends we would have had to place the social identification of Nne Uko as "barren" causally antecedent to the social objectification of her identity as a dike nwami. Nne Uko's own narrative countermanded any such attempt. The event of the hunt, when she fully embodied the archetype of the dike nwami and was proclaimed by her community as such, was an actualizing moment when her identity became socially objectified. This was not just Nne Uko's conviction but was shared by other people with whom I discussed her life.

I tried to get Nne Uko to go into more detail about what she meant when she said she was supposed to have been a man. I wanted to find out if it concurred with notions I had previously encountered in other interviews pertaining to reincarnation or prenatal agreements. While she readily asserted that she believed in reincarnation, she did not identify with a particular ancestor. Nor did she elaborate her case in relation to a specific cosmological model. She preferred to leave it on the level of the manifestly apparent: that her proclivity to move in the masculine domain was evidence of a prenatal disposition that diverged from her biological endowments.

Nne Uko's conviction that her own unique achievements were the result of a cosmological disjuncture is consistent with Jackson's (1989:60) observation that "a 'belief' in external independent agencies or powers seems often to be a necessary precondition for people to assume responsibility for their own situations and destinies." However, the notion of destiny, as understood in Igbo cosmology, must be distinguished from the notion of structural determinism as understood in the social sciences. If one accepts Durkheim's position that gods are merely personifications of social forces, then the two notions do, at first appearance, bear a family resemblance. In Igbo cosmology each person has a shadow guardian known as *chi* that accompanies him or her through life. Prior to birth, individuals negotiate their life path with their chi and, in some views, with the great Chi (*Chi-ukwu*) or God. Other interests such as ancestors also get involved, and reincarnated spirits may have agendas of their own drawing upon prior life experiences. In some cases troublesome spirit entities also get mixed up in the procedures. Some people arrange to be rich, others poor, some to live to an old age, others to succumb early.

There is little to be gained by trying to find a logic in these otherworld conferences. What is of importance is that in the Igbo view destiny is neither entirely chosen nor completely given. It is *negotiated*. Uchendu (1965:15) has written that to the Igbo, "The world is a marketplace and it is subject to bargain." He goes on to add: "This description of life in the idiom of market exchange is not a mere theoretical formulation of mine; it is the Igbo way and is manifested in their everyday behavior." Ultimately the Igbo cosmology is not deterministic at all. One's destiny is negotiated in a crowded primordial palaver; but even then, it is merely a contract, subject to betrayal. Misfortune may be interpreted as either the unfolding course of destiny or as a result of having strayed from one's destiny. Choice emerges at each turn, and people are always able "to act otherwise" (Giddens 1986:14). When Nne Uko addressed her ancestors she told them:

It was you who prepared me to act.
I am not acting on my own power.
It is by the power you have given me that I act.
My father and mother raised me to live as they lived.
(Awa 1991a:19-A-01)

In saying this she is not disavowing the ability to act on her own but rather affirming the Igbo assumption that good life comes only when one acts by way of the sanction of one's ancestors: "to live as they lived." This is the persuasive rhetoric of ritual oration; again a negotiation, aimed at acquiring the requested blessings. In the Igbo view, social constraints constitute a dominant aspect of the ground upon which one's life is played out, but they cannot determine its outcome. The social grounds undergirding Nne Uko's situation were clearly a forceful factor in her unusual life. She was a member of a matrilineage that owned much land and that needed heirs to secure its holdings. The fact that Nne Uko had no children constituted a dilemma for her maternal descent group, a blockage in the system of property distribution, and a disjuncture in social continuity. But this fact was not enough to explain her particular life-project. Nne Uko revealed that as her life unfolded she experienced a growing sense of her manly character and preordained destiny as divergent from that of most women. The event of the ritual hunt, the extraordinary divine intervention, and Nne Uko's bold performance were crucial in gaining public recognition and acceptance of this personal sense of herself. Hence, when she didn't become pregnant she was not treated like other barren women who were compelled to make sacrifices to ancestors and fertility shrines to remedy their condition. She had sought another path for herself: that of the dike nwami.

## Female Husbands

"Female husbands" are well documented in the anthropological literature on Africa. Early in the century Meek (1925:209) referred to the practice as "a curious and ancient custom" among the Yoruba, Nupe, and other groups in northern Nigeria. Other early reports included Thomas (1914:59) and later Talbot (1932:195–96) on the Igbo in southeastern Nigeria, the Seligmans (1932:164–65) on the Dinka and Nuer in the Sudan, Stayt (1931) on the Venda in the Transvaal, and Herskovits (1937) discussing the practice in Dahomey. These accounts treated woman-to-woman marriage as an ethnological curiosity that highlighted particular features of kin-based social and economic organization. Later studies by Evans-Pritchard (1951:107–9) on the Nuer and Gluckman (1950:184) on the Zulu provided additional data but few new insights. With the florescence of anthropological theory in the 1960s (Ortner 1984) the topic was revitalized, and woman-to-woman marriage became a reference point in the controversy regarding the relationship between gender and power in Africa.

O'Brien (1977:112–13) identified two "types" of female husband. The first consisted of women who acted as surrogates for their deceased fathers or nonexistent brothers in order to provide heirs for their agnatic lineage. The second category included "autonomous female husbands": women who married independently to improve their social standing and sometimes to have children when they themselves were infertile or postmenopausal. While general agreement existed regarding the circumstances conducive to woman-to-woman marriages there was considerable disagreement as to the gender status of female husbands. The crux of the debate was identified succinctly by Oboler (1980) who asked, "Is the female husband a man?" Were female husbands socially reclassified as males—a fudging of gender categories for structural purposes—or were they evidence of a broader base of female social potential in these societies?

O'Brien (1977:120–21) observed that among the southern Bantu "females who assume positions of power are expected to become social males." In support of this contention she observed that such female leaders were prohibited from marrying men. Rivière (1971: 68) argued that women who marry other women were always conceptualized as male, and thus for analytical purposes such marriages need not be considered distinct from male-female unions. Data from other regions, however, suggested that such broad generalizations could not be made. Huber (1969:746) observed that among the Simbete, women who marry in this manner are not considered men, or even husbands, but are referred to by the women they marry as "mother-in-law." A stronger criticism came from Krige (1974:32–33) who argued that while in some societies a transposition of gender may accompany woman-to-woman marriage, in others, such as the Lovedu where women exercise considerable political and jural au-

thority, the right to marry women is as much a feminine as a masculine prerogative.

The critique was most clearly formulated by Obbo (1976:371)
who noted that ideologies of male dominance in Africa were too
often mistaken for a social reality. The bias toward male informants
and male idioms of social exegesis led ethnographers to depict
woman-to-woman marriage as an anomaly that was tolerated because it resolved certain structural discontinuities. In contrast to this
view she provided case studies illustrating that woman-to-woman
marriage was one of several strategies women employed to overcome
the limitations imposed by dominant male ideology. Obbo (385)
made the observation that "while African women seek and utilize
the options available more on an *individual* basis to secure maximum
personal benefit, Western women by contrast seem more determined to liberate womankind . . . through collective organization"
(italics in original).

I question Obbo's essentialized "Western" and "African" strategies. Certainly many examples can be cited of collective mobilization
against male authority by African women (e.g., Ritzenthaler 1960;
Van Allen 1972; Mba 1982) as well as the employment of individual
strategies against male dominance by women in the West. Obbo's
observation does, however, expose a theoretical bias that charac-
terizes both sides of the debate. Because the focusing has been on
the implications of woman-to-woman marriage for models of social
organization and our understanding of "women's roles" in particular
societies, little attention has been given to how individual female
husbands create, conceptualize, and explain their own lives.

Just as researchers tend to naturalize ideologies of male dominance, they also naturalize ideologies of Western dominance by assuming the primacy of formal analytical models in interpreting non-
Western cultures. The narratives of our informants and the personal
and cultural exegesis emerging from those narratives are generally
treated as "data" rather than forms of reflexive theorization in their
own right. As we increasingly acknowledge that ethnography is a
socially and historically embedded process, the categorization of academic discourse as objective theory and indigenous discourse as subjective data becomes suspect (Fabian 1983:160; Jackson 1989:3–5;

Turner 1992:15–17). I propose that powerful interpretive frame-works may be found in the perspectives of the people we study. While social theorists emphasize the primacy of the social over the individual and of structure over agency, our informants tend to explore the play of structure, contingency, and the character of individuals in interaction. Their narratives embrace that complex and irreducible whole that constitutes lived social praxis.

## Revolution or Restoration?

While women in Ohafia, like Igbo women in general, have considerable social mobility and economic autonomy, they are, nevertheless, subject to culturally defined divisions of labor, space, and activities on the basis of sex. But against the daily formality of gender there are ritualized moments during which women are allowed, even encouraged, to engage and compete in those endeavors that are normally used by men to establish the strength and courage which is said to constitute masculinity. One example of this is the Ụzọ Iyi ceremony that takes place every other year in the village of Elu. Young maidens hoping for fertility in their marriages, and older women suffering barrenness, make sacrifices to Ishia, a fertility shrine associated with a local spring. During the ceremonies the girls replicate the proud posturing of boys, engaging in wrestling matches and shouting insults at everyone who comes near the makeshift tower they erect in the village square—particularly older men.

Rituals of reversal such as this occur in many cultures and have received much attention from anthropologists. In Max Gluckman's classic analysis of Zulu ceremony he argues such inversions of relations perform a kind of functional catharsis. In order to supplicate an earth goddess and gain good harvests, young Zulu girls dress as men and, fully armed, take cattle to pasture as men normally would. Later in the ceremonies, women and girls go without clothes, singing lewd songs and shouting insults at the men they meet. Gluckman concludes that this ritualized "domination" of men by women provides them a temporary cathartic release from their subservience while reinforcing a sense of the "normal rightness" of the social order that constrains women at other times (1965:116). Peter Rigby (1968:153) suggests that Gluckman exaggerates the rebelliousness of Zulu rituals. Rigby's analysis provides a detailed examination of how ritual inversions are structurally related to ritual objectives. He argues that manipulation of gender roles, including armed women displaying "warlike behavior," is considered by the Ugogo to act as a force capable of affecting sympathetic reversals in misfortunes such as barrenness in women or crop failure (172–73).

Judith Hanna (1977:122) has proposed that both Gluckman and Rigby rely too much on the assumption of the "normal rightness" of male dominance. She observes that Ugogo women seize control of ritual processes at exactly the point at which male ritual specialists appear to have failed.

> Perhaps these representations of conflict through role reversal and behavioral inversions are posited as a latent system of potential alternatives if contingency so warrants: a role reversal in fact, revolution or anarchy. (123)

It is this "latent system of potential alternatives" offering the possibility of "a role reversal in fact" that seems most relevant to Nne Uko's circumstance. Nne Uko's role reversal, which was publicly enacted in the context of a ceremonial hunt, became a role reversal in fact. Her recognition as a dike nwami overflowed the specific bounds of ritual and came to define her social status in life. This, however, did not result in revolutionary change on a social level. Rather, it was an example of the remarkable ability of individuals to manipulate the social order and to achieve a kind of social objectification of their own experience by cultural means.

Unlike the routinized ritual inversions referred to by Gluckman and Rigby, Nne Uko's case seems to be the product of a coincidence of serendipitous events and the will of an exceptional individual. For Nne Uko, to become recognized as a dike nwami was both to become recognized as a *man* (albeit in a woman's body), and also to become a fully realized *woman* by means other than biological motherhood. In this manner she was ultimately able to claim and fulfill her role as a senior elder woman in her maternal descent group. The "normal rightness" of the social order that Gluckman saw affirmed by Zulu rites of reversal was, in Nne Uko's case, not merely reinforced but was *reconstituted*. The reversal of fate, which Rigby saw as the motivation of the Ugogo rites of reversal, was not merely the objective of an irrational ritual of sympathetic magic, but ultimately resulted in a reversal of fate *in actuality:* Nne Uko's "barrenness" was overcome by social rather than biological means, and she became a grandmother.

The inseparability of social structure and human agency becomes clearly manifest in Nne Uko's life. This is an important realization for social theorists, but, perhaps more vitally, it is a basic tenet of the Ohafia worldview. The Ohafia would concur with Sartre (1969:45) that "in the end one is always responsible for what is made of one." Regardless of how often individual Ohafia people may give credit to God, ancestors, and other "external agents" for their successes and failures, in the end, as every burial ceremony makes clear, each person ultimately takes the credit or blame for whatever he or she has or has not accomplished during life. When death takes Nne Uko, the ceremony will celebrate her accomplishments, her children's age-sets will perform, and the men of the Ekpe society will dance in her honor. Her successes will be acknowledged in grand style. When she is lowered into the grave, however, a small incision will be made in her womb so that "it will be open" in her next incarnation.

Nne Uko became a heroine because she prevailed in her life. As an ancestress honored in the ududu shrine she will be remembered for generations, her name invoked and her blessings sought by those seeking the success of crops and the birth of children. She obtained this honor not by pretending to be something she was not but by daring to be what she truly was: a dike nwami, a brave woman indeed.

CHAPTER 7

# Sacrifices for Chike

Countless people have sought the origins of sociology in
Montesquieu and Comte. That is a very ignorant enterprise.
Sociological knowledge (savoir) is formed rather in practices like
those of the doctors.

(Foucault 1980:151)

I remember vividly the first time I met Chike. I was walking
along a dirt path through the village of Amaekpu. A motorcycle was
bounding rapidly down the path toward me, and I hopped the deep
erosion ravine that meandered along the center of the road so as not
to be in the line of the cyclist. Chike was riding on the back of the
motorcycle: immaculate, dressed in a black European business suit.
When he saw me he forced the driver to stop and began to call me by
name: Mr. McCall! Mr. McCall! Being conspicuous as the only for-
eigner in Ohafia and a common topic of idle conversation and gos-
sip, I was accustomed to strangers who seemed to know me. But
strangers dressed in black suits who addressed me formally in English were often troublesome agents from the State Security Service,
and the stern look on his face suggested that I should brace myself
for yet another encounter with bureaucratic harassment. Instead,
Chike quickly informed me that he was the brother of Patience,
junior wife to my friend Ink. I told him that I was on my way to see
Ink at that very moment, and he responded that he too would be at
Akanu later that day and that I should tell Ink to expect him. His
hard gaze melted into a smile, and he said that he had heard much of
me and that he would soon be getting to know me well. "I'll see you
at Akanu," I said, turning back down the path as he sped away.

By then I had already heard of Chike. Ink had told me that he
was concerned about this brother of his junior wife. He had been the
brightest hope of his parents. Quick at his studies, he easily gained
entrance into the university and acquired a degree in accounting, a
certification which, in Nigeria, almost guarantees employment at

high wages. But he had lost a succession of jobs in various distant cities. He had finally been hired as chief accountant for the hospital at Afikpo, not far from Ohafia. For the first time in years he was in frequent contact with his family. Within Chike's family there was a growing concern over his behavior. Ink recounted his own concerns regarding Chike: "I saw the man spend 3,000 naira in one day on trifles; a radio, a tape player . . . And all the while he was paying back loans to people or arranging to borrow money from others." According to Ink, this type of behavior, characterized as "money passing through one's hands," often foreshadowed a chronic loss of control of one's life. I had heard many tales of people who had been thus afflicted. A malady of the successful, it always began with seemingly trivial excesses. If it was allowed to continue, the victim sometimes was reduced to a helpless beggar.

## Chike's Mother's Mother

In addition to being a schoolteacher and the secretary of the local chapter of the Nigerian Teachers Union, Ink was a highly skilled *dibia*, a traditional doctor.[1] Earlier that week I had been at Ink's home near his school in the village of Elu where he lived with Patience during the workweek, returning to his "true" home in his natal village of Akanu on weekends. On the evening Patience's maternal grandmother, Nnenne, visited, she was worried about Chike. She discussed his problem with money and his excessive drinking. Her greatest fear was that he would lose his job at the hospital. Clearly, the form of madness from which he seemed to be suffering, characterized by an unstable relationship with money, was a particularly dangerous malady for a professional accountant. Nnenne wanted Ink to arrange a divination session so that the cause of Chike's behaviors could be determined and corrective measures prescribed. Ink insisted that he needed to discuss the matter with Chike first before he made any attempt at healing him.

The fact that Chike's grandmother had consulted an in-law needs some explaining. Normally, in cases such as this, a dibia outside the family would be consulted. But Ink's relationship with this family had begun on professional terms. Ink met Patience when they began teaching at the same school in Elu. At that time she was a troubled woman who often failed to show up to work due to various ailments. As Ink came to know Patience he learned that she was being "treated" by members of an obscure cult from the city of Aba. She was giving nearly all of her salary to these "exorcists" who would come to her house to chant, burn incense, and perform various rituals to banish the demons that they identified as the source of her problems. Ink decided that he needed to intervene, and he drove out the exorcists, inspiring in them the kind of fear that only a dibịa can evoke. He then undertook to treat Patience himself. All this occurred during the period of my research in Ohafia, and I witnessed her transformation. She changed from a gaunt, anxious person to a robust and cheerful one, with a jocular and charming sense of humor. Through the process of the healing Ink and Patience became fond of one another and eventually got married. Patience's relatives were full of gratitude to Ink for the evident good he had done for their daughter. Therefore, he was the obvious person with whom to begin consultation about Chike.

## The Interview

When I arrived in Akanu that morning, Ink's senior wife, Chinyere, told me that Ink had been "working the garden" since before dawn. By the time I reached him, the gradually intensifying heat of the tropical sun was making further work impractical. Clad in a cloth wrapper, sweat, and a thin coating of red dust, Ink proudly showed me the long rows of yam mounds he had planted that morning. As we returned from the garden plot I told him of my encounter with Chike. Ink remarked that he was pleased that Chike was responding to his invitation because he needed to assess the man's attitude toward his own predicament before he could make any decisions regarding how to proceed. Later that afternoon Chike arrived. He and Ink settled in the sitting room of Ink's compound. I feigned disinterest, burying my face in a book, and listened intently.

Drifting back and forth between Ohafia Igbo and English, Chike

described the situation at his job: the hospital had never had a professional accountant before, and the books were extremely disordered
when he arrived. He confidently proclaimed that he alone understood the hospital's accounting system, that he also held the title of
internal auditor and was personally responsible for delivering bank
deposits. He chuckled smugly as he intimated that the hospital man-
agers held him in awe. Whether or not Chike was, in fact, in a
position to embezzle money with impunity it was clear that he believed he was. Chike expected Ink to be impressed by his claims. In
the current era, countless experiences of bureaucratic graft in everyday life have led many young Nigerians to imagine that a position
that allows one to embezzle and extort without fear of retribution
is the very definition of success. Ink began tactfully, reminding him
that he should not be in a rush to gain money, that he had a position
that could lead to substantial wealth but the premature greed would
only lead to an inevitable fall. He then begin to question Chike
about his recent excessive expenditures. "Where did the money
come from?" Chike became visibly uncomfortable and replied: "This
is Nigeria!" thus invoking the most common euphemism for the
cynical marriage of national identity and official corruption. He insisted that his misappropriations were negligible. When Ink maintained his skeptical gaze Chike finally broke and began blurting out
almost mechanically: "You know that my faith is in our Lord in
Heaven, Jesus Christ, who died for our sins . . ." and so on.

Old men in the village often expressed contempt for the Christian credo that "we are all sinners." It lacked the immediate and merciless reckoning of traditional morality. Instead, one could "sin all week
and then find forgiveness on Sunday." Traditionally, "sin" or *arụ* was
mediated by *arụnsi,* literally, "to poison sin." Arụnsi dwelt in ancestral
monuments, certain shrines, natural features like streams, trees, or
caves, or even in particular masks. Wherever arụnsi was, priests or
priestesses presided over the sacrifices made to maintain it and the
negotiations by which it was engaged to punish wrongdoers. Arụnsi
offered no forgiveness, only swift and decisive punishment. Trans-
gressors were struck by lightning or fell ill and died. In addition, other
less esoteric consequences traditionally fell upon wrongdoers, such as
drawn-out community deliberations and ceremonies of public humil-

iation or even exile or slavery. The Christian ethos, with its doctrine of forgiveness and redemption, rested uncomfortably amid a traditional sense of a swift and merciless execution of justice.

It must be pointed out that, from the beginning, Chike's family never considered his problem to be one of criminality. The behaviors were not interpreted as necessarily being wrongful actions so much as they were seen as symptoms of his descent into a particular behavioral disorder, the cause of which would need to be determined by way of divination.

Ink closed the meeting by lecturing Chike at great length about his responsibilities, particularly to his family. He chastised him when he nervously began to light a cigarette: "Your constant smoking and drinking are a disgrace." Chike's family had sacrificed greatly to put him through school. They had poured their limited resources toward his progress. It was now time for him to reciprocate by living with dignity the life for which his family had sacrificed so much. Despite the clear evidence that Chike was beginning to fall, Ink suggested that Nnenne not seek a diviner until he could see how Chike's behavior was affected by this direct confrontation. We did not have to wait long. Rumor reached us that Chike had shown up to work drunk, left in the company car, and gone to a local bar where he proceeded to buy numerous "rounds for the house." Nnenne urged Ink to seek professional help, and in response Ink arranged a meeting with the master diviner Kalu Ibe Okereke.

## The Consultation

I had spent the night at Ink's compound. It was Saturday morning and *Eke-ukwu,* market day in Akanu. As we sat, chewing kola in the shaded hilltop yard, the sounds of the market floated on the breeze: voices shouting and calling, a distant music of drums, bells, and singing, the occasional hum of taxis from other villages bringing *ndi afia,* market people, a phrase that means both buyers and sellers.

Ink explained how the igba aja that was to take place that morning would identify the cause of Chike's behaviors. He assumed that there were three possible sources of the problem. First, the behaviors exhibited by Chike might simply have been his destiny, the life course that he had chosen prior to birth. Second, he might have been under the malevolent influence of another person. Last, he might have strayed from the path of his destiny, bringing these problems upon himself by his own ill-considered actions. Through ịgba aja these alternatives were to be subjected to a process of elimination. Then the specific cause and the appropriate sacrifice could be determined. When Chike's grandmother arrived, the three of us walked together to Kalu Ibe's compound. Kalu Ibe had long since come to welcome my curiosity regarding his work, and after ascertaining that Nnenne had no objections, Ink had arranged for me to sit in on the ịgba aja. Kalu Ibe lived near the village commons, and to reach his compound we passed directly through the market, which was in full swing by the time we reached it. The air was full of the marketplace: the pungent odors of palm oil and fish; the cacophony of hundreds of voices raised in greeting, laughter, and argument; the radiant colors of the cloth worn by the market women. As we passed the palm wine hut that bordered the narrow pathway into Kalu Ibe's compound the men inside began to gesture, as they always did, for Ink and myself to join them. But when they saw Ink's subtle nod toward the Nnenne they recognized that we were coming on business and let us pass.

Kalu Ibe greeted us solemnly, and after a short wait in his sitting room he led us to his Agwụ ụlọ. Every dibịa family keeps a shrine to Agwụ in their compound. Agwụ ụlọ means "home Agwụ" as opposed to Agwụ ọfịa, or "bush Agwụ located in fragments of feral bush near the edge of the village."[2] The Agwụ ụlọ consists of a small room with an altar space, or *ifu Agwụ. Ifu* can mean "face" or "to face." Hence *ifu Agwụ* can be interpreted to mean either "the face of Agwụ or the location where one can "face" or interact with Agwụ.

We took our shoes off before entering the shrine. When we were all inside and seated Kalu Ibe removed his trousers and shirt and put on a ragged wrapper or "george" of India madras. He donned his dibịa hat, a white knit cap covered with cowries and porcupine quills. He sat and opened his *okpogo,* the dibịa toolbox, which held a central position in the ifu Agwụ, and assembled the necessary instruments of his trade on the ground before him: the blood blackened

*ọfọ Agwụ* or dibịa staff, a piece of natural chalk, and a small calabash
bowl containing the afa chains used to perform ịgba aja. He poured
the afa chains onto the floor and picked from among them a thin
chain necklace bearing a small crucifix that he put around his neck.
Then he laid the chains out in three straight lines and prompted
Nnenne to place a ten-naira bill on the floor next to them. He gave
her the piece of chalk and told her to bless the bill with it while
stating the name of the person whom the problem concerned.
She scratched the stone sending a shower of chalk dust onto the bill
and spoke Chike's name. Kalu Ibe then took the chalk himself and
began forming a pile of white dust next to the chains as he performed an incantation to Agwụ requesting assistance for a clear vision of the problem and its solution. He dipped his finger into the
chalk dust and marked his left eye, the distinctive mark of a dibịa.
With the chalk he drew four lines delineating the three chains. As he
drew each line he invoked one of the four market days telling them
to come and take their blessings.

> Eke is our market day in Akanu
> come take chalk
> Orie is Ututu market
> come take
> Afọ is market in [unclear]
> come take
> Nkwọ is Uduma Eze
> come take chalk
> The sacred days are four
> Only a fool says they are eight[3]

Kalu Ibe worked the afa chains for a long time, questioning them,
casting them, and interpreting the layouts, and questioning and casting again. He maintained a low but audible voice and occasionally
would place his finger on a particular shell remarking on its significance. As he interrogated the shells he commented on his readings. At
first he simply described the situation: "he is an educated man,"
"promising career," etc. Then he began to to address the problem
itself. The conclusion was that during his time in school, Chike had

inspired envy in a classmate. This person, who remained unidenti-
fied, had, either intentionally or unintentionally, placed a curse on
Chike that was preventing him from progressing on his path. When
this diagnosis had been arrived at, Kalu Ibe asked for the kaikai that
Nnenne had brought. He handed Ink a shot glass, which he filled and
handed back to Kalu Ibe. Kalu Ibe then poured this into a small hole in
the floor directly in front of the ifu Agwụ. As he did this he invoked
his deceased father, calling him to come and drink and to offer his
assistance and blessings.[4] A second glass was filled, and this was offered to his ọfọ with a similar request for assistance. A third was tipped
onto the floor before him while he called various other ancestors to
come and take their share and offer their guidance. The remainder of
this glass was thrown out the door of the room with a request for
assistance from those who remained unnamed.

Kalu Ibe then began the interrogation of the afa anew. Having
made a diagnosis he now needed to identify the appropriate solution. He distinguished three sacrifices that needed to be made. The
first was to include a cock, an egg, kola, chalk, and a number of other
items. The materials were to be provided by Chike's maternal family
(the family of the querent, Nnenne), but the sacrifice was to be performed in the compound of his paternal family. The second sacrifice
was to consist of a small chick, a large rock of chalk, and a piece of
paper with something written by an unknown hand. These were to
be tied together, taken out to the road, and abandoned. In this case
the paper with writing represented school, the locus where the problem began and the mode of expression associated with it. By extension, the paper was a metonymic token of the curse itself. Hence this
sacrifice was to accomplish the necessary banishing, effectively getting rid of the curse. The last sacrifice involved another cock and
constituted the requisite "settling up" with the ancestors and other
forces that had assisted in the rectification of the problem. As the
sacrifices were discussed, Nnenne expressed a concern that it might
be impossible to get Chike's paternal kin to participate. Chike's father was dead, and his maternal family were not on good terms with
his father's people. In addition, they were Christians and not likely
to agree to participate in a traditional sacrifice. We left the matter in
a state of uncertainty. As it turned out, Chike's grandmother had

trouble arranging the sacrifices, as she had predicted. This fact, and Chike's continued drinking, led her to abandon the project with a declaration that Chike would have to save himself. Chike lost his job, and the last time I saw him he was begging in the streets. His expensive business suit was torn and muddy, and he was, as Ink described it, "completely soaked." Chike did finally "save himself." I asked after Chike in my correspondence with Ink and learned that he eventually got control of his life and his drinking and was holding down a good accounting job in the southern city of Aba.

## The Paradigm of Diagnosis

Prior to our visit to Kalu Ibe's, Ink explained to me the objective of the ịgba aja that was to be performed that day: Given that Chike exhibited behavior that was self-destructive and was creating problems for himself and his family, it was necessary to find the cause. Ink had suggested that there were three possible causes of Chike's aberrant behavior and that the process of ịgba aja would be to identify the specific cause by process of elimination.

The first possibility involved the Igbo conceptualization of "destiny," which is closely associated with the concept of chi. In Igbo cosmology, each individual has a *chi*, a spiritual counterpart and guardian. By Igbo reckoning, certain obligations in life are acquired prior to birth. One of these is an agreement with one's chi called *iyi-ụwa*, literally, "world stream." The term *ụwa* is always used when referring to previous or future "incarnations." The usual translation of *ụwa* is "world," but the Igbo usage suggests a concept of individual "worlds" as *acted in and experienced* rather than a singular objectified "World" that exists external to the person. The metaphor of the stream again utilizes an image of water in transition between the worlds of the living and that of the dead. Just as a spring mysteriously pours forth from the earth and follows its course to the sea, one's "world" comes forth from the maternal womb and, unless diverted, follows its course to death and the realm of ancestors. Chinwe Achebe, in her study of dibịa practices, described the notions of *chi* and *iyi ụwa* as follows:

In Igbo mythology, each individual at birth takes an oath specifying in great detail how he will like to live on earth, all the things he will like to do and become. This oath or '*iyi-ụwa*' is the outcome of an agreement between an individual and his spirit counterpart, the "*chi*." For every individual is imbued with a "*chi*", the creative spark of the ultimate force which creates man and continues the creative process as far as the individual is concerned until the latter goes home to his ancestors and his "*chi*" to his master, "*Chi Ukwu*" in the sky. (Achebe 1986:18)

Ms. Achebe's husband, Chinua Achebe, has pointed out that this notion of a primordial agreement with one's chi implies that each individual is ultimately responsible for negotiating the shape of their own destiny.

It seems there is an element of choice available to him at that point, and that his chi presides over the bargaining. Hence the saying *Obu etu nya na chie si kwu,* which we often hear when a man's misfortune is somehow beyond comprehension and so can only be attributable to an agreement he himself must have entered into, at the beginning, alone with his chi; for there is a fundamental justice in the universe and nothing so terrible can happen to a person for which he is not somehow responsible. (Achebe 1975:165)[5]

Hence any misfortune may simply be a playing out of this primordial agreement. But this should not be taken to imply a fatalism inherent in Igbo concepts of destiny. The chi agreement is negotiated and may be renegotiated. And it is here that the skills of the dibịa come into play. It is also possible that a person can fall into misfortune, because he or she has strayed from the agreed-upon course. Then ịgba aja is necessary to identify the divergence and to prescribe necessary corrections and the appropriate sacrifices with which to appease one's chi.

There is one other type of commitment that can come into play even before the chi agreement is negotiated. In some cases, prenatal obligations may have to do with an oath made in a former incarnation. There is a custom in Ohafia referred to as *ike ụwa,* literally, "to create, or apportion, one's world." A man on his deathbed may call his relatives together and make specific pronouncements regarding his next world. He may indicate that he intends to be born into a particular family. He may also indicate particular goals for his next world.[6] Again, straying from these objectives may lead a person into misfortune.

The second possible source of misfortune is wholly external to the individual. This is the possibility that some person, out of envy or evil intentions, has interfered with one's progress. While it is possible that this may be the product of intentional ritual intervention on the part of one's nemesis it may also come about unconsciously. It is as if the "friction" that envy introduces into the subtle field of social and psychological influences is enough to set the descent in motion.

The final possibility is that no cosmological or occult explanation will emerge. Instead it becomes apparent that the person has brought the problem on by his own failings. In this case the behaviors are not considered as symptomatic of something else but are taken at their face value. They are signs of personal weakness, indications that the person cannot handle the demands and responsibilities in their life and will inevitably "break" under pressure.

### Seeing the Unseen

Glossed in English as "divination," the phrase *igba aja* requires closer examination. The word *aja* occurs in Igbo only in two contexts: *igba aja,* "to divine," and *ịchụ aja,* "to offer sacrifice." The verb *ịchụ* in the latter construction means to "chase" or "drive away." The verb *igba,* found in the construction meaning "to divine," is more difficult to translate because its meaning varies according to context so that it has no true English equivalent. Perhaps the best gloss would be "to engage." Hence *aja* is that subtle agency that is engaged through divination and that is driven away by offering sacrifice. The term *aja* thus embodies a conceptualization that is not adequately expressed when ịgba aja is glossed in English as "to divine." The initiation of a dibia is said to *open the intitiate's eyes,* meaning that the process of initiation enables the dibia to see things that noninitiates cannot.

There were innumerable forms of igba aja employed by diviners in Ohafia. Some involved talking oracles known as *obia.* Others called *ngu* had male and female forms constructed from animal heads and gourds respectively. These hung on strings and answered questions by their movements. Many of the forms of igba aja fell into the category of igba afa, and Kalu Ibe's system was one of these. *Afa* is a kind of seed. Igba afa refers to any form of igba aja using seeds or other kind of small tokens, whether they are afa seeds or not. The system employed by Kalu Ibe used split halves of slippery mango pits tied together with string into chains of four shells apiece. This equipment is similar to that noted by Bascom who found igba afa to be akin to the ifa system used by the Yoruba and to other divinatory systems of southern Nigeria (Bascom 1942, 1969). The flat shells can land either face up or face down thus constituting a binary code. Each chain of four shells can potentially generate sixteen different configurations. In Ifa, a single chain of eight shells is cast but is read as two sets of four resulting in a total of 256 ($16^2$) possible configurations. While shell chains can be found in use by diviners all over southern Nigeria, there are at least two different systems for interpreting them.

The Yoruba ifa system described by Bascom treats each of these configurations as having particular lexical meanings that refer to a body of thousands of oral texts constituting commentaries associated with the configurations.[7] The adept practitioner must have a substantial knowledge of these texts in order to perform adequately, and training requires lengthy apprenticeship and rote memorization.

However, a different system of reading, which did not assign lexical meanings to the configurations or refer to a corpus of established texts, was employed by Kalu Ibe.[8] Rather than using two chains, as is traditional in ifa divination, he used three afa chains, two of which had four cowry shells tied at either end. Cowries were traditionally used as currency. Their presence in sets of four referred to the four days of the market week. These two chains were employed to engage matters in the time of everyday existence, the cowries symbolically alluding to the cycle of the market week and the ebb and flow of material concerns. The third chain had, at one end, two stones referred to as *aka* and *alụ*. I was told that these signified family and land respectively. The opposite end of this chain bore two other stone beads, these being *nkuma mmini* or water stones, taken from a sacred stream. The water stones provided insight into the domain of dreams, and into the realm of water that is at the gateway of the land of the dead. This third chain engaged matters *outside* the time of everyday existence: *aka* and *alụ*, events unfolding in the time of land and family. While an individual may have profited from or even owned land, land survives perpetually. Land is ultimately held, not by people, but by descent groups, maternal and paternal. Hence *aka* and *alụ* represented those dimensions of one's life and identity that came before and persist beyond one's own life span. This chain further engaged the time of dreams, the time of ancestors: the cumulative time that circumscribes all temporal experiences both past and future. The third chain, then, was devoted only to transtemporal influences, those that stood outside the circles of mundane time.

The interiors of the two inner shells of each chain were tinted, one with chalk (white), the other with camwood (red). On the most basic level of interpretation, white signified positive influences and outcomes and red negative, but this simple code became complicated by the position of the shell, which indicated exposure or occlusion. A white shell with its open side up was a good omen. White down indicated that progress was being blocked. Red up indicated that negative influences were present but apparent. Red down suggested that there might be a hidden hindrance. Hence, both positive and negative aspects and potentials were always assumed to be present. The positions of the shells addressed the extent to which they were apparent or hidden. The inner shells carried primary significance. The two shells on the ends of the chain modified the message of the inner shells. If the position of the adjacent shell agreed with the inner shell it strengthened the message; if it was in an opposing position it diminished the significance of the omen. All four shells in an open position was the most auspicious casting: all elements were in their proper position.

The chains were cast in pairs. When I watched Kalu Ibe at work he would cast the two chains bearing cowry shells continuously while interrogating them. When one of these chains indicated a hidden problem he would cast the third chain in conjunction with the chain that had revealed the occult influence and would continue interrogation until a satisfactory understanding of the subtle influences underlying a given situation was achieved.

### "Explaining" Divination

Much of the anthropological literature regarding divination has been concerned with addressing its "logic" and the relationship of that logic to "objective logic" or "rationality." Evans-Pritchard's (1937) classic work on Azande thought and later works by Horton (1964, 1967) and others were characteristic of this concern. This approach continued the Victorian intellectualist assumptions that Frazer (1922) and Tylor (1873) articulated on social evolutionary terms and that Malinowski (1948) problematized by challenging the proposed exclusivity (but not the fundamental validity) of the social evolutionary categorization of "magic, science, and religion." The practical limitations of such analyses have been addressed so broadly and effectively that I will not review the arguments here (see Devisch 1984 and Peek 1991). It suffices to cite Devisch (1984: 67) who argued:

> It is reductionist and irrelevant to require (in accord with a positivistic, scientific paradigm) of divination, or of other institutions forming part of an essentially symbolic world view, that they should produce statements which satisfy the canons of scientific consistency.

Clearly, positing the irrational, nonrational, or quasi-rational status of divinatory practices provides little real understanding of the forms of knowledge engaged by these processes. Rather, a positivist approach to constructing questions about divination is little more than an exercise in distancing subject and object, a bounding of both the reasoning of analysis and the reasoning of the analyzed such that any available grounds for mutual understanding become methodologically excluded.

Some attempts to bridge the positivist epistemological gap have taken the position that diviners and traditional healers practice a kind of indigenous psychoanalysis (see Crapanzano 1973; Edgerton 1980; Prince 1964, 1976). But what assumptions accompany the search for "ethnopsychiatry"? To what extent are the African practices in question, evaluated on the basis of their conformation to a non-African epistemology to which they are said to bear a resemblance? In his conclusion Edgerton argues that the story of the diviner/healer which he has studied "is worth recording simply because he has made an effort to find useful drugs, to continue the beginnings of science within a pre-scientific system of medicine" (1980:93). Thinly veiled in terms like "prescientific," the specter of social evolution haunts these studies that are primarily apologist in character.

The Igbo paradigm that identifies personal, social, and preordained dimensions of one's existence is worthy of consideration on its own terms. If these concepts are stripped of the cultural idioms that frame them, they are not as exotic as they may at first appear. The idea that our fate is shaped and constrained by prenatal arrangement involving ancestors is mirrored in Western conceptions of genetic determinism. The Igbo concept, however, is tempered with the notion of negotiation and the possibility of renegotiation.

This inclusion of negotiability has important consequences. While medical science agrees that a tendency to alcoholism is probably inherited, this knowledge does little to help those thus afflicted. Despite various pharmacological and psychological treatments developed for alcoholics, most professionals acknowledge that the homely existential metaphysics of Alcoholics Anonymous is more effective in helping people cope with their lives in productive ways.

We cannot ignore the existential dimension of conditions evidenced by substance abuse. The Igbo model has appeal precisely because it construes the person, the social, and the preordained as a complex negotiable whole. Western medicine is now readily available to most Nigerians. Government subsidies make pharmaceutical drugs easily accessible, and for the most part Nigerians have eagerly embraced biomedical treatments. Indigenous healers, however, continue to flourish in modern industrial Nigeria. Most healers are registered with the government, but the national healers guild has resisted all attempts to incorporate them into the national health-care system. While indigenous healers commonly refer patients to M.D.'s for treatment of infectious diseases and other illnesses for which the efficacy of biomedical methods is unchallenged, healers are favored in the treatment of what I call "existential disorders." These disorders are maladies of being rather than of body, and they are conditions for which biomedicine provides no solution, indeed, has failed until recently even to acknowledge.

## CHAPTER 8

# Akanu Ohafia and Her Two Founders

$W$hen I first expressed interest in the history of the village of
Akanu, my inquiries were met with polite discouragement. Heated
discussions seemed to explode in my wake, and I soon realized that a
conspiracy to withhold information was afoot. In other Ohafia communities, the stories of the founding father (or, in the case of Ebem,
founding mother)[1] who had first established the settlement were
usually offered without any instigation on my part as soon as I
expressed scholarly interest in the village. I had, in fact, been an-
noyed that some elders seemed to think these stories were all I
needed to know about their community. But in Akanu, obtaining
this basic information was a process fraught with controversy. When
I took this problem to Mr. Ink he provided, as usual, the story behind the story. Ink explained that there were two different histories
of Akanu's founding, and the elders feared that if I were given any
information I would be persuaded, or feel compelled, to accept one
version over the other and publish it in my book as the "true" history of Akanu. This, everyone agreed, would be a disastrous development. The primary concern was not which version was the true or
more accurate account. The problem was the possibility that I might
choose to put one of them in my book and thereby give that account
a higher claim to legitimacy. One might expect that advocates for
the different versions would have competed for my attention in
hopes that their interpretation would be favored. Instead, most people seemed to agree that any attempt to publish either history would
have deleterious effects on relations within the community. There
was an underlying sense that neither of these versions of the past
was altogether adequate in and of itself and that recording history in

a fixed written form created particularly onerous problems for those who would have to live with the consequences.

As I investigated further, I found that even more than two versions of Akanu's founding existed. They all, however, gravitated toward one of two veridical poles, which effectively ascribed seniority to two different patrilineal descent groups: one located in Amafor quarter, the other in Ekelogo. In practice, the primacy of Ndi Agbo compound of Amafor was affirmed whenever a community-wide ceremony was held. Ritual oration constantly reiterated this seniority. A powerful reminder of this was Kalu Akanu, the tutelary arụnsi of the entire village, which had located in Amafor just next to the main meetinghouse before construction of a Presbyterian church near the site necessitated its removal to a more concealed location in Amafor. A large mound of earth remains as a reminder of Kalu's presence.[2]

There were, however, certain spatial cues that seemed to suggest another possible configuration. The ogo in front of the meetinghouse in Amafor was so small it was inadequate for public events in a community of several thousand inhabitants. Ogo Ekelogo, on the other hand, was large and shaded by old trees. On market day it was Ogo Ekelogo where market women gathered to sell their produce, and the large ogo was the site of many village events. The village itself curves in an S shape following a meandering ridge. The top of this curve falls in steep precipices; on one side is a valley containing a bountiful spring that provides Akanu with excellent pure water. The four quarters of the village lie along this ridge starting with Ekelogo, then Amafor, Ndi Odo, and finally Utugokoko. When masqueraders perform they must always follow this serpentine route, dancing first at Ekelogo and then to Amafor and so on through the village in the order that the various ogos occur on route. I wondered, is this sequence random or can it be read like a cumulative stratigraphy recalling the order in which the ridge was settled?

The area between Ogo Amafor and Ogo Ekelogo was originally a section of virgin bush that was protected by severe ritual sanctions. The presence of a patch of "bad" bush (*ọfia ọjọ*) in the center of a village is a common configuration in Igboland. The Scottish Presbyterians who established their mission in Akanu in 1910 built a massive stone church on this site, supplanting the sacred powers associated with the location with their own sacred authority. Thus at the heart of the village three powerful markers of power lie in a line vying for attention: the meetinghouse of Ekelogo with its large commons and market, the massive Presbyterian church, and finally the small meetinghouse of Amafor where a mound of earth near the ogo reminds all that the powerful Kalu Akanu resides there.

My friend Jakus assured me that the history of the village had already been written by his late father nearly three decades ago. I was delighted. His father, Ajike Kalu Ume, was one of Ohafia's early literate intellectuals who had been a pioneer in writing in the Igbo language. I was translating his book, *Ohafia Dike n'Agha* (Ume 1960), into English and was interested to see his account of Akanu's founding. When we arrived at Jakus's uncle's compound to retrieve the document we were told that the document was lost—eaten by white ants. Jakus was visibly disappointed, and I resolved to accept yet another failure to capture Akanu's elusive history. Several years later, however, while doing archival research at the University of Cambridge I found a copy of Ume's (n.d.)[3] history of Akanu in the files of the late G. I. Jones, who had solicited such histories from village elders all over Igboland. Jones, in his wisdom, had collected not one, but both histories of Akanu, one favoring Amafor, the other Ekelogo. The history supporting Amafor's primacy was written by Okoro Odachi (1965) who was at that time head of Ndi Agbo Amafor and by official reckoning chief of Ohafia. Jakus's father's history presented the antithetical account according primacy to Ekelogo.

Odachi's history begins by citing an earlier document prepared by District Officer C. J. Mayne in 1931 as part of a British colonial intelligence report. The document was based on information provided to Mayne by Akanu elders in his office in Bende. Mayne's text is quoted at length and tagged with the words "Extracted from File No. 94/1931, Certified True Copy, District Interpreter, Bende Division, 31/8/62." According to this account, Akanu was founded by Odowukwu,[4] who was forced to flee from Elu after he committed a murder. He wandered from place to place for some time before founding a new home at what is now Ndi Agbo compound in Amafor Akanu. Odachi provided additional information, including an account of the founding of Ekelogo quarter explaining that it was "given" by Odowukwu to Nnaukwu Omezua, his "maternal relative"[5] who "ran away from Elu with him." Another telling of these events, offered to me by an Akanu man who requested anonymity, reverses this exchange. In this version, Nnaukwu Omezua settled Ekelogo first and "gave" what is now the neighboring Amafor quarter to his brother, Odowukwu, who was also his elder. In this case, the principle of primogeniture prevailed over the principle of first settlement, thus transmitting the right of primacy to Ndi Agbo Amafor. In either case the foundership goes to Amafor.

One of the notable features of Ume's alternative history of Akanu is the complete absence of the otherwise illustrious (and notorious, in Elu at least) Odowukwu. In Ume's version, a man named Agbai Ukwu was the first settler, though we must consider that this may be a variant name Odowukwu. He established himself at what was to become Amafor but then "deserted the settlement before the arrival of Nnaukwu" at Ekelogo. According to Ume, Agbai Ukwu returned later to "claim foundership and headship of the village." Nnaukwu contested this claim, and the whole dispute was taken before the high tribunal of elders at Elu who, according to Ume, awarded headship to Nnaukwu. The contentious battle for foundership won Nnaukwu and his people the moniker *umu akanugh* or "stubborn people." This, shortened to *Akanu*, became the name by which the community was known. In his account of Amafor, Ume mentions that it was eventually settled by a man named Agbokenta "who was the 8th to settle here with Nnaukwu." This is mentioned presumably because he was the founder of Ndi Agbo, the senior compound of Amafor.

The conclusion that my book would present a problem if I was allowed to publish a history of Akanu was clearly a product of this series of written histories beginning with Mayne's in 1931. The two accounts written for Jones in the 1960s assign the village headship to two different quarters with such certainty that they appear irreconcilable. The elders in Ohafia were well aware of the problems created by writing history down. Mayne's history had been used to support one of the later versions. I still have no idea what intrigues lay behind the fact that Jones was also given a copy of the alternative history, but I can only suspect that Ume was attempting to neutralize the impact of the growing textual fixity of the other version. It might seem at first that these contradictory histories presented a problem to be resolved. In fact the variant histories play a crucial role in the villagers' knowledge of the past and their use of this knowledge in the present. Most of the time these divergent knowledges were kept out of each other's way. At times of crisis, however, such alternative knowledges have been mobilized to undermine the expansion of authority and reconstitute the autonomy of the constituent sections of the community. When alternative interpretations of the past were evoked in the heat of a discussion over issues of concern to the whole community it signaled those in authority that the time had come for compromise. As I explored Akanu's past I became less concerned with what the "true" history of the community was, and I also realized the naïveté of trying to ascertain what people in Akanu "believed" their history was. Rather, I was confronted with an argument against writing the history at all. This position was based in an instrumental theory of history that framed it as a complex, indeterminate body of narratives, the significances of which change as they are brought to bear upon issues in the present. By codifying history as text we run the danger of extinguishing other explanations of the past and with them the possibility of rethinking history and the incipient power inherent in that possibility.

The skepticism toward writing history that I encountered in Akanu suggests a model of history as contingent, indeterminate, and subject to endless interpretation. This may seem a rather "postmodern" notion to find operative among rural farmers in southeastern Nigeria. It must be observed, however, that this understanding is a product of interactions with a colonial authority in which written histories were introduced as a means to imbue the structurally amorphous, "acephalous" communities of the region with a political rigidity rendering them capable of integration into the coercive system of British indirect rule. Ohafia concepts of history and its uses follow from indigenous practices representing history in dynamic oral and performative media. A history that is "danced" produces a distinctly different order of knowledge than one that is codified in text.

This book's title, *Dancing Histories,* is intended to suggest two

interpretations. It refers first to the fact that in Ohafia, representations of history are frequently presented as complex performances
including music, dance, singing, costume, and masks. Thus, histories are danced—and historical knowledge is constituted and maintained through performance. The title can also be read as a poetically
rendered theoretical statement that history has many aspects, many
trajectories, many possible renditions. That is, we are faced with a
dance of multiple histories—the products of contingent events, social forces, and human agency all refracted through the interpretive
lenses of those choreographers we call historians. Lastly, the title
*Dancing Histories* should be understood to imply an intimate relationship between these two interpretations.

The Heuristic ethnography is the methodological path that has led
us from danced history as an ethnographic event to the analogy of a
dynamic interplay of histories. This was accomplished by assuming
that the activities, events, relationships, and exchange of ideas that
constituted ethnographic research not only produced ethnographic
data but also offered a uniquely appropriate source of theoretical
models. When, in 1989, I first traveled to Ohafia, Nigeria, to conduct
ethnographic research, my fundamental concern was to gain a better
understanding of the relationships many Ohafia people maintained
with their ancestors. At that time, I assumed that these relationships
were primarily expressed and enacted through ritualized events conducted by elderly men and women according to clearly prescribed
ceremonial protocol. I did find, in fact, a robust culture of ancestor-
related ritual in Ohafia. I also found, however, that there was a
broader basis of knowledge about ancestors that was constituted in
the experience of daily life. This knowledge was not solely the concern of elders, shrine priests, or ritual specialists but was also a matter
of common everyday experience. I went to Ohafia expecting to find
a cosmological basis for ancestral beliefs. What I found was a perva-
sive ancestral presence constituted primarily, not in cosmology, but
in practice—not in belief but in the lived experienced of the quotidian world.

This experiential core, grounded in everyday life, provides the
epistemological framework in terms of which interactions with an-

cestors are not only made possible but become crucial operations in the construction of the Ohafia people's identity and their understandings of the past and its significance. Rather than examine these understandings as a closed "belief system" that precludes critical or theoretical reflection, my analysis has assumed that the possibility for such reflection is integral to the knowledge in question. To identify and utilize these critical perspectives theoretically we must recognize that they too are grounded in the experience of growing up and living in Ohafia. This epistemological ground is unique to Ohafia. It is realized through the idioms of Ohafia language and constituted in terms of Ohafia social experience. Ohafia social experience, however, shares a large measure of common ground with human experience in general and is, therefore, potentially accessible to all. My task has been to work through the play of idiom and culture specific to Ohafia to elicit this perspective in a manner that neither mystifies, glorifies, nor denigrates it, but rather makes it intelligible on its own terms to those who have not shared the landscape of knowledge that obtains in Ohafia. This is not a particularly radical goal for ethnography; indeed it is merely a definition of what ethnography has always done. What is more radical is the analytical role I have assigned to the indigenous concepts of the social world.

Traditionally in anthropology the ideas, practices, and utterances of the people whom we study have been confidently located in the category of "data," while we have reserved the "theoretical" arena for our own ideas and methods and those of our fellow researchers. These two perspectives have been analytically isolated and are often glossed as "emic" and "etic," borrowing from the linguistic distinction between the paradigmatic characteristics of a particular language and the characteristics of languages in general. When applied carelessly, this distinction can imply that the people we study lack the intellectual tools to reflect critically upon the relations and processes that social scientists study. This assumption of a kind of ontological privilege for academic researchers effectively alienates them from the discourse within the culture they study. If anthropologists are to move beyond the broad but ultimately shallow reductions of evolutionary, functional, economic, and structural explanations it is crucial that we engage intellectually in the worlds that we seek to explain. As long as anthropologists remain committed to a discourse *about* the people they study rather than a discourse *with* those people, they will find themselves masters of the trivial and will seem increasingly irrelevant in the emerging multicultural world. This book has been a modest attempt to think and act otherwise.

# Igbo Orthography

Several orthographic systems have been developed for Igbo and its dialects. Scholars such as Uchendu (1965) and Ottenberg (1968, 1989) use a system of phonetic symbols that predate the International Phonetic Alphabet (IPA). Nsugbe, in his ethnography of Ohafia (1974), employs Union Igbo orthography (sometimes called the old orthography) developed by missionaries for Bible translation. The system I use for Ohafia Igbo follows the Standard Igbo orthography prescribed by F. C. Ogbalu (1981) that is now employed in Igbo language instruction in Nigeria. However, words and texts are rendered in Ohafia dialect and not in Ogbalu's synthetic Standard Igbo dialect. Certain characteristics specific to Ohafia dialect should be noted. In some contexts, such as the word *ọfụfụ,* the sound indicated by the character *f* may be spoken as an aspirated bilabial fricative (IPA: ɸʰ). In addition, *s* as in *isi* may sound as i<u>sh</u>i, i.e., an unvoiced post-alveolar fricative (IPA: ʃ). These are traditional Ohafia pronunciations, and they are increasingly considered obsolete by Ohafia speakers as instruction in Standard Igbo dialect reduces regional variations. All Igbo dialects are tonal, and linguists recording Igbo texts often represent tone contours as well as using double vowel characters to distinguish long vowels. I, however, follow Ogbalu in not using diacritical indications of tone or vowel length. I have, however, chosen to make a few practical exceptions. I render proper names without diacritics when such spellings have precedence of use: hence, *Agwu* rather than *Agwụ,* and *Amafor* rather than *Amafọ.* Azuonye (1974, 1983) renders his informants' names phonetically including double characters to indicate vowel length, e.g., *Kalu* is written *Kaalụ.* In reference to Azuonye's informants I have taken the liberty of restoring their names to the common spellings that are almost certainly the forms most familiar to them. Most consonants approximate the values they have in English. The diagraphs *gb* and *kp* represent voiced and unvoiced bilabial implosives respectively, *gh* represents a pharyngeal fricative (IPA: ħ). The symbol *ṅ* represents a velar nasal stop (IPA: ŋ) as in so<u>ng</u>.

All Igbo dialects use eight vowels, and a variety of symbols have been used to represent them. The following chart indicates the symbols used herein (Standard Igbo) and their equivalents in other systems.

**Igbo Vowel Character Equivalents**

| Standard Igbo (Ogbalu) | International Phonetic (IPA) | Ottenberg and Uchendu | Union Igbo (Nsugbe) |
|:---:|:---:|:---:|:---:|
| a | a | a | a |
| e | ɛ | ɛ | e |
| i | i | i | i |
| i̟ | ɪ | e | i |
| o | o | o | o |
| ọ | ɔ | ɔ | ọ |
| u | u | u | u |
| u̟ | θ | θ | θ |

# Notes

## Chapter 1

1. Kaikai is a locally produced form of distilled alcohol.
2. Ekpe society employs a complex iconology of secret gestures and signs known as *nsibidi* or in Ohafia as *nsibiri*. Basic gestures, which are used for identification and proof of membership, are taught during initiation. Knowledge of other signs can be gained in various ways. The total inventory of nsibiri is vast. Once one is taught the fundamental basis of syntax and semantics it is possible to learn nsibiri by watching adepts as they interact, challenging one another's knowledge of the system. Particular nsibiri have multiple meanings that correlate with degrees of initiation. Thompson's (1963: 173–87) examination of the Ngbe society (Ngbe is the name by which Ekpe is known among the Ejagham) includes one of the best discussions of nsibiri to date. However, it should be noted that the Ejagham use the term *nsibidi* to refer only to the written signs and refer to the performed signs as *egbe* (Thompson 1963: 180). The Ohafia use the term *nsibiri* to refer to both forms. Various researchers have published "translations" of ideographic nsibiri (MacGregor 1909; Dayrell 1910, 1911; Talbot 1912:448–61; Cole and Aniakor 1984:61). These are first-order iconic interpretations and do not touch upon initiatory knowledge. See chapter 4 for additional discussion of Ekpe.
3. Azuonye's dissertation (1974:490–94) includes a different version of this same tale. In this variant the boy, known simply as Ebele, is sent to war, not by his age-mates, but by his father. When he returns victorious his parents have no wealth with which to celebrate so his mother resolves "to fete her son with a song of joy from her heart" (*abụ obi ụtọ*).
4.

Ibe-a Kamalu bịa ṅụrụ mmanyị!
Ikpang Ukwu bịa ṅụrụ mmanyị!
Okwun Ibe Aja bịa ṅụna mị mmanyị!
Akpọtụ Nna ukwu Omezue Uwa ọbịa ngwa ngwa!
Ike mmadụ zu ọfịa wụ ọnwụ!
Odo Awa ukwu bịa nụna mị mmanyị!
Ibe Imaga ṅụrụ mmanyị!
Umachi Ajike bịa, anyị nọa mmanyị, ya gị onye ọgụ!
Alị Ohafia Ezema, Onye ga ubi ọrụ ji ya lụa!
Onye ga ude ọnụma ya lụa!

Ọga ọfịa egbe ya lụa!
Ọgụ beri beri, ma onye asọkwa asọ!
                                    (Mmuko 1991:25-A-01)

5. The question of the "rationality" of "other" (i.e., not European science–based) "systems of thought" has a long history in anthropology dating at least from Frazer's (1922) "theory of magic" and Levy-Bruhl's (1923, 1926) essays on "primitive mentality," which focus on the exotic character of what was imagined as the non-Western mind. Later writers such as Malinowski (1948) and Evans-Pritchard (1937) review this approach critically and go on to explore the functional coherence of specific systems of belief and practice while maintaining that Western science has a unique claim to objective observation. Robin Horton (1970) systematically develops this particular argument in his classic essay "African Traditional Thought and Western Science" in which he draws many parallels between "African thought" (represented primarily by divination practices) and science as it is practiced in European and American academies. Horton's primary conclusion is that Western science is distinguished from African practices because it is "open" to revision while African practices such as divinatory techniques are bound by tradition and are "closed" to change. This argument, indeed the entire tradition preceding it, has been criticized as employing an ahistorical caricature of African thought. Critics such as Mudimbe (1988), Appiah (1992), and eventually Horton himself (see Appiah 1992:127) have recognized that the tradition-bound, change-resistant model of the posited "African system of thought" was a product of the limits of functionalism rather than any putative African mentality.

## Chapter 2

1. Ink's careful wording suggests the subtle and often misconstrued status of symbolic action in ritual practice. There is a tendency for analysis to become bogged down in the exercise of verification or falsification of occult practices and thus miss the point regarding the relationship of these actions to the very real processes of transformation brought about by the ritual itself.

2. *Ịgba aja* usually refers to divination but a closer translation is difficult. The term *aja* only occurs in one other construction in the Igbo language: *ịchụ aja*, "to offer sacrifice." The verb *ịgba* in the former construction means "to engage, to see, to divine." While the verb *ịchụ* in the latter construction usually means "to chase away," some of my informants insisted that in the context of *ịchụ aja* its meaning was different and that it meant "to appease or conciliate." Any attempt to translate *aja* with an English gloss would move us further from rather than closer to an understanding.

3. Ufie is a red pigment made from the bark of the *abọsị* tree (camwood, *Baphia nitida*). Odo is a yellow pigment made from the bark of the

*okwukwo* tree (*Terminalia superba*). The powder is produced by rubbing bark on soft yellow sandstone, the stone also contributing to the pigment.

4. The noun *ifu* means "face." Like the English term it also serves as a locative meaning "in front of" or "to face." Hence, *ifu Agwu* is the face of Agwu and the point at which one faces Agwu. There is only one Agwu but it has many faces. These faces are made by humans so that they may face Agwu and interact ritually with it.

5. The Igbo market week (*izu*) has four days. These weeks are further categorized into two types designating greater and lesser markets that alternate so that the full market cycle is eight days. In most of Igboland this period is referred to as *izu abụa* (two weeks). In Ohafia dialect this phrase is meaningless. The Ohafia refer to this period as *izu atụ* (three weeks). It appears that this system of enumeration counts the number of markets rather than the number of weeks.

## Chapter 3

1. These syllables (kpaṅ-kpaṅ-kpa . . . ) are an Ohafia vocal representation of the war dance timeline (see note 9, this chapter).

2. The ikperikpe ọgụ is a small wooden membrane drum about 20 cm in diameter tapering to about 15 cm at the base and about 40–50 cm in height. The head is antelope or other wild animal hide held fast by long strips of plant fiber affixed to a woven fiber ring near the base of the drum. This ring is held in place and tightened with tapered wooden wedges. The ikperikpe is the most common form of drum in Ohafia, and various sizes are used in different musical contexts. There is a traditional women's jural association that is called *ikperikpe* due to their ritual use of this instrument (see Nsugbe 1974:67–68). In more casual contexts, such as school ensembles, modernized ikperikpe constructed with nylon clothesline rather than plant fibers are common. The ikperikpe ọgụ, however, must be made of traditional materials. The war dance is sometimes referred to as ikperikpe ọgụ, which suggests the importance of the voice of the drum in the overall performance.

3. The *opu* (antelope horn trumpet) is known as *opi* in other Igbo areas.

4. Men often use this call to rally a crowd prior to a speech or performance. *Kwe nụ* roughly translates as an imperative form of "agree" or "consent." Utugokoko is the section of the village in which the performance is taking place, Akanu the village itself, which in turn is a part of Ohafia, which is one of many regions of Igboland, etc. Hence this oratory invokes groupings of collective identity beginning with the most local and proceeding in leaps of concentric inclusion to the national level.

5. This comment was made to me by Joseph Agara of Ndi Uduma Amoke, Ohafia. The idiom "*nkwa ebrilọkụ*" meaning "the music takes fire" indicates the point at which full intensity is achieved in a performance.

6. Ohafia's neighbors, the Aro, were an integral part of Ohafia's martial history. See chapter 4 for further discussion.

7. Drewal (1992:12) uses the term *spectacle* to translate the Yoruba term *iran* that refers to performance complexes including music, dance, visual display, and drama. The term *egwu* is probably a more exact Ohafia/Igbo equivalent to *iran* than is the term *iri*.

8. A story of one such heroine is recorded in chapter 6.

9. The term *timeline* refers to a fundamental rhythmic pattern (usually played on a bell, block, bottle, or other idiophone). This nomenclature follows Stone (1988:43) who notes alternate terms used by other scholars of African music such as "structural core" (Kubik 1983:38), "timekeeper" (Nketia 1958:21), and "standard pattern" (King 1960). The iri agha timeline can be transcribed as follows:

The syllables at the beginning of this chapter (*"kpań-kpań-kpa-kpań-kpań-kpa-kpań-kpań-kpa . . ."*) are an Ohafia vocalic representation of this rhythm. Such vocables are never sung in performance but serve as an aural system of notation.

10. The drummed phrase "A- gwọ ntụ nọ a- ka-rị- ka!" uses two tones.

(Agara 1991:17-A-00)

11. While membrane drums are capable of a wide range of sounds depending on stick and hand techniques, other instruments, such as the double bell *ogele* (*ogene* in northern Igbo areas), are less capable of sound articulation. The minimum requirement for instrumental speaking is that the instrument must be able to produce two notes that are easily distinguishable as low and high tones. The interval should be at least a whole tone and preferably a minor third or greater.

12. Ure is a popular women's dance; like iri agha it includes a dance leader carrying a headdress. Instead of carved heads, the ure headdress features carved figures called *nwebe*. Nwebe are associated with rites for the increase and restoration of female fertility.

13. It should be noted that the term *tempo* is used here to refer to the meter of the music as well as the speed. The first (masculine) rhythm, here spoken in vocables, is that of iri agha and iri ekpe transcribed in note 9. The second (feminine) rhythm, which is played more slowly, transcribes as follows.

14. Electric fishes inhabit streams in the region. Hence, the term for electric shock predates the advent of electric generators.

15. This participation occurs at varying degrees and trajectories of involvement. The overlap of shared experience and knowledges allows the possibility of collective knowledge. The contingent quality of individual histories and variant experience constitutes the dynamic and indeterminate quality of social process. Thus the "reciprocity" referred to by Merleau-Ponty is characterized by both continuities and disjunctions.

16. Relevant to this discussion of the ontologization of social relations in time are Clifford Geertz's comments on Alfred Schutz's (1971:17) conceptualization of "predecessors," "consociates," "contemporaries," and "successors" as spatial/temporal divisions within the aggregate category "fellowmen." Geertz (1973:366–67n) notes:

> where "ancestor worship" [is] present, successors may be regarded as (ritually) capable of interacting with their predecessors, or predecessors of (mystically) interacting with their successors. But in such cases the "persons" involved are, while the interaction is conceived to be occurring, phenomenologically not predecessors and successors, but contemporaries, or even consociates.

17. Mbiti (1969:23) makes a similar observation regarding African conceptions of the past in his discussion of the Swahili word *Zamani*, "[*Zamani*] is the final storehouse for all phenomena and events, the ocean of time in which everything becomes absorbed into a reality that is neither after nor before."

18. Certeau (1986:4) uses this phraseology to propose that psychoanalytic theory offers a striking antithesis to historiography's "clean break between the past and the present," noting that the approaches employ "two different ways of distributing the *space of memory*" (italics in original). I am not proposing that iri agha is akin to psychoanalysis in any therapeutic sense. They are exercises of a very different order; psychoanalysis engages a personal, interiorized, and repressed past while iri agha constitutes a collective, exteriorized, and expressed past. The relevant of Certeau's observations is to emphasize that the historian's conception of the past is one of many possible perspectives, even in the view of the human sciences.

19. Chernoff's notion of "African aesthetics" is questionable to the extent that it suggests an essentialized "African culture." However, I consider his critique of the limits of objectifying interpretations of African performance to be valid.

20. Ite odo took two forms: first, a large pot that was filled with palm wine for the celebration of new trophy heads; and second, the pot bearing heads that was used as a headdress. The priest of ite odo was the guardian of both these pots and saw to their appropriate use. The society of proven warriors was also called *ite odo*.

21. Preparation of heads was performed under the supervision of the priest of the ite odo (see previous note). All trophy heads were soaked in a large bowl called *nja nsi* that contained a special tincture of herbs. The flesh was removed and copper rings were often attached to the sides for display purposes. The nja nsi was kept behind the village *ikoro*, a massive slit gong that was used to communicate important announcements regarding deaths, declarations of war, and the celebration of warriors.

22. I saw the ite odo carried for the burial of His Royal Highness Ezie Okorie Kalu Uma in May 1989. This occasion was the only time during my stay in Ohafia that I was asked not to take photographs.

23. These caps are identical to a European tam, even to the detail of the pompon at the top. Similar hats are now ubiquitous in southern Nigeria but only those with the distinctive pattern of black, white, and red stripes are recognized as Ohafia war caps.

24. For an excellent discussion of Cross River notions regarding the human acquisition of leopard qualities see Thompson (1963:186–87). Space does not allow a full discussion of leopard societies in the Cross River region. However, certain distinctions should be noted. The well-known Ekpe (Ekpo, Egbo, Ngbe) society that is now centered in Calabar was and continues to be very active in Ohafia. *Ekpe* is Efik for leopard. The Ekpe society extends throughout the Cross River region and even beyond. Its members come from many different language and ethnic groups but ceremonial songs are still sung in Efik. Ekpe is not a warriors' society. It is primarily involved in jural and occult activities.

25. Customarily, when a baby boy cuts his first tooth neither the mother nor father will comment publicly on the matter. They will wait until the auspicious event is noted by a friend or relation. Sometimes this is even prompted by the mother who may complain that the baby has something wrong with his mouth and will ask the friend to examine him. Once it is announced that the baby has "cut his first head" the bearer of this news is responsible to sponsor the celebration of the event. The cutting of first teeth is also celebrated for baby girls. However, it is not referred to as "cutting a head," and the celebration is not as elaborate as that for boys. Instead it is said that "she has asked us not to go to the farm," because the family must stay home from work in honor of the occasion (Kalu 1991c:16-A-00).

26. Smaller birds, which make the most difficult targets, are the most highly valued. A boy might meet ridicule if he kills too large a bird. The *nza*, a type of hummingbird, is considered to be the best. The boys seek out a type of flowering shrub called *obolo-nza* (hummingbird flower), which, as its name implies, is frequented by hummingbirds The boy conceals himself next to the flower and waits for the bird's appearance. The hunt requires patience but if the boy persists and remains quiet he will be able to shoot the nza at very close range (Kalu 1991c:16-A-00).

27. Ottenberg (1989:42–45) records a similar practice in Afikpo.

28. *Perere pere ja* are onomatopoeic words derived from the sound of the bird's wings. The original Ohafia text is as follows:

Onye? Onye gbara ogbe? Ogbe!
Onye? Onye gbara ogbe? Ogbe!
Pusa ife gba nkoko? Ogbe!
Nkokoya epugh abuba! Ogbe!
Perere pere ja! Ogbe!
Pere ja pe ja ja! Ogbe!

29. In Ohafia initiation rites for girls had largely fallen out of practice by the time Nigeria gained independence in 1960. Clitoridectomies were traditionally performed shortly after birth as were male circumcisions.

These operations were somewhat perfunctory and were performed without the ritual elaborations often associated with circumcision in Africa. Because of the absence of symbolic significance attached to circumcision, when medical clinics became established in Ohafia, medical doctors rapidly assumed responsibility for male circumcisions and the practice of female circumcision was abandoned (Kalu 1991c:16-A-00).

30. I acquired both a traditional bow and arrows and a market slingshot and practiced with them in the enclosed yard of my compound. With the slingshot I quickly learned to hit small targets at distances up to fifty feet. The bow and light reed arrows were very difficult to manage, and even when I had modified the arrow, fletching it with chicken feathers, I never learned to extend my effective range beyond about twelve feet.

31. This is in marked contrast to the Ilongot notion of head-hunting. According to Renato Rosaldo, Ilongots view head-hunting not as incorporation but as its opposite.

> To take a head is, in Ilongot terms, not to capture a trophy, but to "throw away" a body part, which by a principle of sympathetic magic represents the cathartic throwing away of certain burdens of life—the grudge an insult has created, or the grief over a death in the family, or the increasing "weight" of remaining a novice when one's peers have left that status. (1980:140)

# Chapter 4

1. Dike's (1956:153–62) discussion of the *Order of the Blood Men* records the British campaign to eliminate the ritual sacrifice of humans in Calabar.

2. Land tenure is based on a system of double unilineal descent similar to that of nearby Afikpo, which has been authoritatively described by Ottenberg (1968). Most agricultural land is held by the matrilineal descent groups while residential property and some gardens close to the villages are held by patrilineal descent groups. An ethnography of Ohafia was published in 1974 by Phillip Nsugbe who served as the Nigerian government ethnographer and antiquities officer for the region from 1962 to 1964. Nsugbe attempted to challenge Goody's (1961) classification of Ohafia kinship as a system of double descent, arguing instead that Ohafia should be considered matrilineal. Most of the evidence presented by Nsugbe, such as platitudes regarding the reverence for mothers in Ohafia and his discussion of the quality of maternal and paternal kin relations, is irrelevant to the formal argument. The weakness of Nsugbe's position is clear in his discussion of comparative attitudes toward maternal and paternal relatives. He employs Lévi-Strauss's (1976) model, which predicts that fathers will tend to be indulgent toward their sons in matrilineal societies, while relations with the mother's brother will be more authoritarian. Hoping to use this contention to support his argument for Ohafia matriliny, he states, "In Ohafia the

relationship [mother's brother and sister's son] is one of unfamiliarity tinged with veiled mutual hostility" (Nsugbe 1974:84). He contrasts this with the patrilineal Igbo claiming that their relations are the inverse. Nine pages later, Nsugbe seems to have forgotten this structural argument and stressing the importance of the matrilineage writes, "True as it is that the deepest feeling of warmth and welcome awaits the Ibo man in his mother's brother's household, it is even more so for an Ohaffia Ibo [*sic*]" (93). The only evidence in Nsugbe's argument that addresses the criteria defined by Goody is the fact that Ohafia patrilineages are not strictly exogamous. In practice, the larger matrilineal unit, the *ikwu*, is not always strictly exogamous either, a fact that Nsugbe overlooked. In any case, there seems little to be gained from underestimating the importance of patrilineal relations in Ohafia for they are substantial. If Goody's criteria were too rigid to account for Ohafia's marital arrangements this does not detract from the fact that Ohafia provides an excellent example of a society organized on a principle of double unilineal descent.

3. Various forms of ịgbandụ rituals were used in Ohafia. All of them were public rituals conducted by village or lineage elders. Here were three common forms:

> 1. The two people entering into the ịgbandụ relationship would be given palm kernels, and as they chewed them they would take vows of allegiance. Leaves of an *abọsị* tree (camwood, *Baphia nitida*) would be arranged on the floor, and when they had sucked the oil from the kernels and completed their oaths they would drop the chaff on the leaves, which would then be cast into the latrine.
> 2. Each ịgbandụ party would be given a small cut and their blood mixed in a small cup of palm wine or kaikai. Each would state their vows of allegiance and then drink of the mixture.
> 3. A kola nut would be blessed and cut into sections. Each ịgbandụ party would be cut and given a piece of kola. Taking their vows, they would put their own blood on the kola, pass it to the other party, and both would chew the kola. (Kalu 1991a:10-B-02)

4. In other parts of Igboland the names *Abam* or *Ada* were used generically to refer to the Aro's armies, which often included Edda Abam and Ohafia men fighting together. The Ohafia and the Abam claim a common ancestry and share many cultural attributes including double unilineal descent and the war dance.

5. Darwin (1871:192) in the *Descent of Man* wrote: "At some future period, not very distant as measured by centuries, the civilised races of man will almost certainly exterminate, and replace, the savage races throughout the world." Of African "history" the American Du Chaillu (1867:437) wrote: "That [the Negro] will disappear in time from his land I have very little doubt; and that he will follow in the course of time the inferior races who have preceded him. So let us write his history."

6. The Anglican CMS did not venture as far as Ohafia, which was first

missionized by a Scottish Free Presbyterian missionary, Reverend Collins, in 1912.

7. In 1893 it was renamed the "Niger Coast Protectorate" but was generally referred to as "Southern Nigeria."

8. Dike and Ekejiuba (1990:159) suggest that the attack on Obegu resulted from a breakdown in the debt collection system that the Aro had traditionally enforced on behalf of their trading partners.

Obegu traders, encouraged by the growing influence of the British authority were beginning to challenge Aro traders who had controlled the trade between their territory and the coast. Their refusal to pay the debt owed to Akwette people as a result of an earlier system was on the belief that the British could intervene to prevent seizure of debtors and their property.

Oral accounts suggest that the warriors at Obegu were primarily from Abam and that only a few Ohafia participated.

9. An abridged version of Eke Kalu's autobiography was published in the journal *Nigerian Field* (1936).

10. Dane-guns were muzzle-loading rifles prized by the Ohafia warriors at that time. Lead shot was rare and copper too valuable to waste as ammunition. Short-ranged, inaccurate, and loaded with pebbles or even corn, these weapons were not particularly lethal and depended more on their ability to scare the opponent.

11. Ndukwe insists that the grave of this officer is located in Ebem.

12. Personal communication (1990).

13. Customary practice prohibits villagers from working their farms on their village market day. Hence, boys and girls would be available for other labor.

14. Eke Kalu (1954:9) relates a similar argument for schooling in his autobiography:

There was in Ohafia one Vincent, a Seirea [*sic*] Leonean, who was the Native Court Clerk. He was extremely wicked in his dealings with the Ohafia people. On one occasion he locked several of them in the prison yard for a trivial cause. They broke out and were intent on beating him when he instantly reported the matter to Major Cobham. The latter promptly dispatched policemen to his rescue. Later fines were imposed on the people. My people wanted a way out of such persecution and my advice to them was to open a school, educate their children who, knowing what the clerk knew, could better challenge him and his successors.

15. It should be noted here that the waylaying of travelers was not previously an acceptable means of obtaining heads. Ajike was driven to such marginalized activities because he continued to pursue head-taking after the socially legitimized means to do so had ceased to exist.

16. Aside from his "return from the dead," Nna Ajike's story has an-

other notably legendary aspect. Music's power to overwhelm people, influencing them to take reckless actions, is a standard motif in Igbo folklore. For instance, the hero tortoise (*mbe*) was known to use this method to lure lambs to the slaughter. However, it would be careless to assume that this folkloric element implies fictionalization in the story of Ajike. Ajike's story only illustrates that the power of music expressed in Igbo folklore is a fact in Igbo life.

17. Translated from Ume's original Igbo text by the author and Ibe Ukoha Ogboso.

18. This quote comes from an interview about events in Ohafia during the Biafran conflict. The Ohafia man who provided the interview requested anonymity.

## Chapter 5

1. Uchendu's model of ancestors in Igbo cosmology is indistinguishable from those produced by Igbo theologians (Ilogu 1973; Obiego 1984; Metuh 1985; Okorocha 1987). These works are primarily devoted to arguing a fundamental commonality between Christianity and Igbo traditional belief. In this view ancestors are structural intermediaries between humans and the supreme god (Chukwu). Nwoga (1984) has criticized this self-referencing body of literature on Igbo religion, arguing that the notion of "Supreme God" was introduced to the Igbo by missionaries. He suggests that the importance of ancestors in Igbo ritual is seriously distorted by studies devoted to constructing a model of Igbo religion based on a Christian paradigm of doctrine rather than indigenous practice.

2. Alma Gottlieb's (1992:46–71) discussion of "Double Descent as a System of Thought" resurrects the notion of lineage precisely *because* it closely resembles the Beng people's own practice of using kinship as an idiom of social identity. Ancestors, however, apparently have little importance in Beng society so Gottlieb's study does not address the problem at hand.

3. Thompson (1963:28) also refers to "ancestral presence" in some forms of African art, music, and dance.

4. The oko tree (*Pterocarpus soyauxic*) is known as ọha in Umuahia. In the Anambra valley it is called ọra.

5. Traditionally, Ohafia women retained their fathers' names throughout life. In recent times, however, the European practice of taking the husband's "surname" has become common.

6. In other parts of Igboland the patrilineage is called *umunna* (children of the same father) rather than *umudi* (children of the same husband). The latter is identified from the wife/mother's perspective rather than that of the children or father. In Ohafia *umunna* refers to a grouping of several related umudi. Ohafia's matricentric terminology may be related to the importance of maternal descent in Ohafia, a characteristic that distinguishes it from most other Igbo groups. The Ohafia term for the immediate

matrilineage is *umunne* (children of the same mother). The more extensive matriclan grouping is called *ikwu*.

7. Ohafia terms for "lineage" refer to groups of people of common descent that are concretized in terms of residential space occupied and utilized. This model differs from the anthropological notion of lineage, which invokes the image of a "line" or "tree" extending through time. A spatialized conceptualization of ancestry seems to be common in African societies. Michael Jackson (personal communication, 1989) has observed that Evans-Pritchard (1940a:202) remarked on this distinction but failed to heed the epistemological implications.

8. The Ohafia term *moṅ* is cognate with the terms *mmọụ, mmọ, mmọnwụ,* etc., in other Igbo dialects. However, in Ohafia it is used only to refer to *ancestral* spirits and not to bush spirits or other entities as are cognates in other regions.

9. In some cases the ọnụ ogo is referred to as *ezi* while in umudi is called *ime ezi.* Nigerian government literature identifies the iso ogo as a "ward" or "hamlet." Nsugbe (1974:40) eschews official and indigenous terms and refers to the isi ogo as the "primary division," the ọnụ ogo as the "secondary division," and the umudi as the "tertiary division."

10. This concise statement of the ritual instrumentality of the Ọkwankọ performance was made by Ohafia indigene Dr. J. Akuma Kalu Njoku of Ohafia who is currently teaching in the United States.

## Chapter 6

1. The long basket was traditionally used by women to carry produce but when bearing heads it would resemble the headdress worn by the leader of a war dance troupe.

2. No one, including Nne Uko, knew her exact age. My estimate is based on information about her age-set and the fact that she indicated she was a young woman when the Igbo "Women's War" occurred in 1929.

3. Yams are a "men's" crop, and yam titles are usually only held by men even if the labor that contributed to the production of the yams was provided primarily by their wives or mothers.

4. Libation oration situates events in social and historical space. The orator calls the names of male ancestors in the paternal line associated with the host compound entreating them to come and join in the drinking. Skill at libation oration is judged by one's knowledge of ancestral names and a facility with proverbs. Nne Uko's oration was excellent in this regard.

5. When girls reached puberty they were secluded in "fattening houses." They ate rich foods and were exempted from farm labor so they could become voluptuous in preparation for marriage and childbearing. This custom has not been practiced in Ohafia since the 1950s.

6. This "pygmy" antelope or duiker (*Cephalopus mergens*) is known as *mgbada* in other Igbo areas.

7. I asked a shrine priest who had had such a visitation about the

form of the entity. The priest said it is very difficult to describe, that it is not anthropomorphic but like the presence of "a kind of darkness."

8. While sexual abstinence and prolonged nursing were the most common forms of birth control in Ohafia at that time, abortifacients were available from herbalists.

9. This type of "bride purchase" is distinct from conventional bride negotiations in several ways. The bride wealth required is much greater, and on contractual and practical levels it resembles the buying of a slave more than it does the wedding of a wife. However, if a woman thus acquired is ever referred to as a slave, she can charge the offender with having gravely insulted her and will be entitled, by customary law, to recompense.

10. O'Brien (1977:109) notes that:

nowhere do the Africa data suggest any homosexual connotations in [woman-to-woman] marriages. Rather, the wife of a female husband chooses or is assigned one or more males who become her sexual partners and the biological fathers of her children.

11. An Ekpe chief confided to me that Nne Uko was allowed to initiate specifically because she was barren. He noted that she never passed beyond the lower ranks. Despite the fact that her membership may have been limited I was assured by the chief that when she died, the Ekpe masquerade (Okonko) would perform at her burial as it does for all members.

## Chapter 7

1. The term for traditional doctor in Ohafia dialect is *bibịa*. I have used the Central Igbo form, *dibịa*, because it is better known and is now in common use even in Ohafia.

2. *Agwụ* is the name of the force that empowers dibịa to heal (see chapter 2).

3.

Eke wụ afịa anyị Akanu
bịa gwere nzụ
Orie wụ afịa Ututu
bịa gwere
Afọ wụ afịa (unclear)
bịa gwere
Nkwọ wụ Uduma Eze
bịa gwere nzụ
ụbọchị nze di anụ
onye ibiribe sị ọ dị asatọ

Uduma Eze (line 7) is the founder of Ohafia. The central market for Ohafia is held on Nkwụ day in Elu, the village that he founded.

4. The presence of this hole indicates that Kalu Ibe's father was buried directly under the floor of this room. The hole is considered to lead "directly to his mouth," and libations offered for him in that room will be poured into this hole.

5. The proverb roughly translates as "it is as he and his chi said it would be."

6. Ink is an example of such a case. Ink's father's eldest brother died without producing any children. He pronounced on his deathbed that he would reincarnate as the next son to Ink's father. He said that this lack of offspring was the sorrow of his life and that in his next incarnation he would father many children. Shortly thereafter, Ink's mother became pregnant, and Ink was born. Now, forty-some years, three wives, and fifteen children later, Ink could only smile and say, "I think that I am living up to my goal."

7. Bascom includes transcriptions of some of these texts in his work (1969). Judith Gleason has, in conjunction with John Ogundipe, collected many of the ifa texts as recounted by Awotunde Aworinde (Gleason 1973). The original recordings of these are deposited in the Archives of Traditional Music at Indiana University (3).

8. I in no way want to give the impression that Kalu Ibe's method of reading afa constitutes a typical "Ohafia" system. In fact, while I noted a great variety of forms of igba aja in use by dibia in Ohafia, I know of no other dibia who employed afa chains. Dibia strive to employ as many exotic techniques for healing and divining as they can afford to acquire, and it is likely that Kalu Ibe learned this method while traveling in a distant region or from someone else who had obtained it thus.

## Chapter 8

1. The village of Ebem is said to have been founded by a woman who was banished from the village of Elu because it was feared she would give birth to twins. Twins were greatly feared as dangerous anomalies, and the banishing of twin mothers was customary in those days. Twin children were killed, usually by abandonment. The women who gave birth to them often suffered the same fate but were sometimes kept alive by their relatives though forced to live in complete isolation. Residing alone in the woods, the banished woman of Ebem gave birth to a single son. When the error was realized, her husband begged her to return but she refused, preferring to stay "ebem," literally, "down there" on the lower end of the ridge south of Elu (which means hilltop). The ruling family of Ebem is said to descend from this woman. Ebem is the only village in Ohafia that claims a woman as founder.

2. Kalu or Kamalu is the arunsi associated with lightning and thunder.

3. The document in question is signed Ajike Kalu. I refer to him as

Ume herein for consistency because in his other cited work he uses the full name—Ajike Kalu Ume.

4. Mayne renders this name as "Odawku." Odacahi clarifies this error, explaining that the name is a contraction of Oda Awa Ukwu.

5. By "maternal relative" Odachi means the two men belonged to the same *ikwu* (matrilineal descent group).

# References

Recorded interviews are referenced in the text by the name of the interviewee followed by the date of the recording and a control code in the following format: tape number-side-track. The recorded interviews cited here have been deposited at the Archives of Traditional Music, Indiana University, Bloomington.

Achebe, Chinua. 1975. "Chi in Igbo Cosmology." *Morning Yet on Creation Day*. Garden City, NY: Doubleday.

Achebe, Chinwe. 1986. *The World of Ogbanje*. Enugu, Nigeria: Fourth Dimension.

Afigbo, A. E. 1981. *Ropes of Sand: Studies in Igbo Culture and History*. Ibadan: Oxford University Press.

Agara, Joseph. 1991. 17-A-00. Recorded interview and demonstrations of instrumental language.

Appiah, Kwame A. 1992. *In My Father's House: Africa in the Philosophy of Culture*. Oxford: Oxford University Press.

Apter, Andrew. 1992. *Black Critics and Kings: The Hermeneutics of Power in Yoruba Society*. Chicago: University of Chicago Press.

Arua, A. O. 1951. *A Short History of Ohafia*. Enugu, Nigeria: Omnibus Press.

Awa, Uko Uma. 1991a. 19-A-01. Recorded oration.

———. 1991b. 19-A-02. Recorded interview.

Azuonye, Chukwuma. 1974. *The Narrative War Songs of the Ohafia Igbo: A Critical Analysis of their Characteristic Features in Relation to Their Social Function*. Ph.D. dissertation. University of London.

———. 1983. "Stability and Change in the Performances of Ohafia Igbo Singers of Tales." *Research in African Literatures* 14 (3): 332–80.

———. 1990. "Kaalụ Igirigiri: An Ọhafịa Igbo Singer of Tales." In I. Okpewho, ed., *The Oral Performance in Africa*. Ibadan: Spectrum Books.

Barnes, J. A. 1962. "African Models in the New Guinea Highlands." *Man* 62:5–9.

Bascom, William. 1942. " 'Ifa Divination': Comments on the Paper by J. D. Clarke in Journal of the Royal Anthropological Institute, (59:1939)." *Man* 42:235–56.

———. 1969. *Ifa Divination*. Bloomington: Indiana University Press.

Ben-Amos, Paula. 1976. "Men and Animals in Benin Art." *Man,* n.s., 2 (2): 243–52.

Blacking, John. 1973. *How Musical Is Man?* Seattle: University of Washington Press.

———. 1979. "Introduction." In J. Blacking and J. W. Kealiinohomoku, eds., *The Performing Arts: Music and Dance.* New York: Mouton Publishers.

Bourdieu, Pierre. 1977. *Outline of a Theory of Practice.* Cambridge: Cambridge University Press.

Brain, James L. 1975. "Ancestors as Elders in Africa—Further Thoughts." *Africa* 41 (2): 122–33.

Calame-Griaule, Geneviève. 1965. *Words and the Dogan World.* Philadelphia: Institute for the Study of Human Issues.

Certeau, Michel de. 1986. *Heterologies: Discourse on the Other.* Minneapolis: University of Minnesota Press.

Chernoff, John. 1979. *African Rhythm and African Sensibility: Aesthetics and Social Action in African Musical Idioms.* Chicago: University of Chicago Press.

Clifford, James. 1988. *The Predicament of Culture.* Cambridge, MA: Harvard University Press.

Cole, Herbert M., and Chike C. Aniakor. 1984. *Igbo Arts: Community and Cosmos.* Los Angeles: Museum of Cultural History, University of California, Los Angeles.

Connerton, Paul. 1989. *How Societies Remember.* Cambridge: Cambridge University Press.

Crapanzano, Vincent. 1973. *The Hamadsha: A Study of Moroccan Ethnopsychiatry.* Berkeley: University of California Press.

Darwin, Charles. 1871. *Descent of Man: And Selection in Relation to Sex.* New York: A. L. Burt.

Dayrell, E. 1910. "Some Nsibidi Signs." *Man* 67:113–14.

———. 1911. "Further Notes on Nsibidi Signs with their Meanings, from Ikom District, S. Nigeria." *Journal of the Royal Anthropological Institute* 41:521–40.

Devisch, René. 1984. "Perspectives on Divination in Contemporary Sub-Sarahan Africa." In W. van Binsbergen and M. Schoffeleers, eds., *Theoretical Explorations of African Religion.* London: Kegan Paul.

Dike, Kenneth O. 1956. *Trade and Politics in the Niger Delta.* Oxford: Oxford University Press.

Dike, Kenneth O., and Felicia Ekejiuba. 1990. *The Aro of South-eastern Nigeria, 1850–1980.* Ibadan: University Press Limited.

Drewal, Margaret T. 1992. *Yoruba Ritual: Performers, Play, Agency.* Bloomington: Indiana University Press.

Du Chaillu, Paul B. 1867. *A Journey to Ashangoland.* New York: D. Appleton.

Durkheim, Emile. 1938. *Rules of Sociological Method.* Chicago: University of Chicago Press.

Edgerton, R. B. 1980. "Traditional Treatment for Mental Illness in Africa." *Culture, Medicine and Society* 4 (2): 167–89.

Eke, O. 1990. 13-B-01. Recorded interview.

Evans-Pritchard, E. E. 1937. *Witchcraft, Oracles, and Magic among the Azande.* Oxford: Clarendon Press.

———. 1940a. *The Nuer: A Description of the Modes of Livelihood and Political Institutions of a Nilotic People.* Oxford: Clarendon.

———. 1940b. *The Political System of the Anuak of the Anglo-Egyptian Sudan.* London School of Economics Monographs in Social Anthropology, no. 4. London: Lund.

———. 1945. *Some Aspects of Marriage and Family among the Nuer.* Lusaka: Rhodes-Livingstone Institute Paper No. 11.

———. 1951. *Kinship and Marriage Among the Nuer.* Oxford: Clarendon.

———. 1956. *Nuer Religion.* Oxford: Oxford University Press.

Fabian, Johannes. 1983. *Time and the Other: How Anthropology Makes Its Object.* New York: Columbia University Press.

———. 1990. *Power and Performance: Ethnographic Explorations through Proverbial Wisdom and Theater in Shaba (Zaire).* Madison: University of Wisconsin Press.

Feld, Steven. 1982. *Sound and Sentiment: Birds, Weeping, Poetics and Song in Kaluli Expression.* Philadelphia: University of Pennsylvania Press.

Fernandez, James. 1986. *Persuasions and Performances: The Play of Tropes in Culture.* Bloomington: Indiana University Press.

Forde, D., and G. I. Jones. 1950. *The Ibo and Ibibio-speaking Peoples of South-Eastern Nigeria.* London: International African Institute.

Fortes, Meyer. 1945. *The Dynamics of Clanship among the Tallensi.* London: Oxford University Press.

———. 1949a. *The Web of Kinship among the Tallensi.* London: Oxford University Press.

———. 1949b. "Time and Social Structure: An Ashanti Case Study." In M. Fortes, ed., *Social Structure.* Oxford: Clarendon.

———. 1953. "The Structure of Unilineal Descent Groups." *American Anthropologist* 55 (1): 17–41.

———. 1959. *Oedipus and Job in West African Religion.* Cambridge: Cambridge University Press.

———. 1969. *Kinship and Social Order.* Chicago: Aldine.

Fortes, Meyer, and G. Dieterlen, eds. 1965. *African Systems of Thought.* London: Oxford University Press.

Foucault, Michel. 1980. *Power/Knowledge.* New York: Pantheon.

Frazer, Sir James. 1922. *The Golden Bough.* London: Macmillan.

Geertz, Clifford. 1973. *The Interpretation of Cultures.* New York: Basic Books.

Giddens, Anthony. 1976. *New Rules of Sociological Method.* New York: Basic Books.

———. 1979. *Central Problems in Social Theory.* New York: Basic Books.

———. 1986. *The Constitution of Society.* Cambridge: Polity Press.

Givens, David, and Timothy Jablonski. 1995. "1995 Survey of Anthropology PhDs." *Anthropology Newsletter* 36 (6): 11–12.

Gleason, Judith. 1973. *A Recitation of Ifa Oracle of the Yoruba.* New York: Grossman.

Gluckman, Max. 1950. "Kinship and Marriage Among the Lozi of Northern Rhodesia and the Zulu of Natal." In A. R. Radcliffe-Brown and D. Forde, eds., *African Systems of Kinship and Marriage.* London: Oxford University Press.

———. 1965. *Custom and Conflict in Africa.* Oxford: Basil Blackwell.

Goody, Jack. 1961. "The Classification of Double Descent." *Current Anthropology* 2 (1): 3–25.

Gottlieb, Alma. 1992. *Under the Kapok Tree*. Bloomington: Indiana University Press.

Griaule, Marcel. 1965. *Conversations with Ogotemmêli: An Introduction to Dogon Ideas*. Oxford: Oxford University Press.

Hanna, Judith L. 1977. "African Dance and the Warrior Tradition." *Journal of Asian and African Studies* 12:111–33.

Henderson, Richard N. 1972. *The King in Every Man: Evolutionary Trends in Onitsha Ibo Society and Culture*. New Haven: Yale University Press.

Henige, David. 1982. *Oral Historiography*. London: Longman.

Herskovits, Melville. 1937. "A Note on 'Woman Marriage' in Dahomey." *Africa* 10:335–41.

Horton, Robin. 1964. "Kalabari Diviners and Oracles." *Odu* 1:3–16.

———. 1965. *Kalabari Sculpture*. Apapa, Nigeria: Nigerian National Press.

———. 1967. "African Traditional Thought and Western Science. Part II." *Africa* 37:155–87.

———. 1970. "African Traditional Thought and Western Science." In Bryan Wilson, ed., *Rationality*. Evanston: Harper and Row.

Huber, Hugo. 1969. " 'Woman Marriage' in Some East African Societies." *Anthropos* 63/64:745–52.

Ilogu, Edmund. 1973. "Worship in Ibo Traditional Religion." *Numen* (Leiden) 20 (3): 229–38.

———. 1974. *Christianity and Igbo Culture*. Onitsha, Nigeria: University Publishing.

Isichei, Elizabeth. 1973. *The Igbo People and the Europeans: The Genesis of a Relationship—to 1906*. New York: St. Martin's Press.

———. 1976. *A History of the Igbo People*. New York: St. Martin's Press.

———. 1978. *Igbo Worlds: An Anthology of Oral Histories and Historical Descriptions*. Philadelphia: Institute for the Study of Human Issues.

Jackson, Michael. 1982. *Allegories of the Wilderness: Ethics and Ambiguity in Kuranko Narratives*. Bloomington: Indiana University Press.

———. 1986. *Barawa, and the Ways Birds Fly in the Sky*. Washington, DC: Smithsonian Institution Press.

———. 1989. *Paths Toward a Clearing: Radical Empiricism and Ethnographic Inquiry*. Bloomington: Indiana University Press.

Jones, G. I. 1988. *The Background of Eastern Nigerian History: Oral Tradition*. Vol. I. New Haven: Human Relations Area File, Inc.

Kalu, Eke. 1936. "An Ibo Autobiography." *Nigerian Field* 7 (4): 158–70.

———. 1954. *Autobiography of an Illustrious Son, Chief Eke Kalu of Elu Ohafia, Owerri Province*. Lagos: Pacific Printing Works.

Kalu, Ibe Nwosu. 1991a. 07-A-02. Recorded interview.

———. 1991b. 10-B-02. Recorded interview.

———. 1991c. 16-A-00. Recorded interview.

———. 1992. Letter to the author dated September 4.

Karp, Ivan. 1978. "New Guinea Models in the African Savannah." *Africa* 48 (1): 1–16.

Karp, Ivan, and Kent Maynard. 1983. "Reading *The Nuer.*" *Current Anthropology* 24 (4): 481–92.

Kasfir, Sidney L. 1988. "Celebrating Male Aggression: The Idoma Oglinye Masquerade." In S. Kasfir, ed., *West African Masks and Cultural Systems.* Tervuren: Musee de l'Afrique Central.

King, Anthony. 1960. "Employments of the 'Standard Pattern' in Yoruba Music." *African Music* 6 (3): 51–54.

Kopytoff, Igor. 1971. "Ancestors as Elders in Africa." *Africa* 43 (2): 129–42.

———. 1987. "Introduction." In I. Kopytoff, ed., *The African Frontier.* Bloomington: Indiana University Press.

Krige, Eileen J. 1974. "Woman Marriage with Special Reference to the Lovedu—Its Significance for the Definition of Marriage." *Africa* 44:11–36.

Kubik, Gerhard. 1983. "The Emics of African Musical Rhythm." Unpublished manuscript.

Kuper, Adam. 1982a. *Wives for Cattle.* London: Routledge and Kegan Paul.

———. 1982b. "Lineage Theory: A Critical Retrospect." *Annual Reviews of Anthropology* 11:71–95.

Leith-Ross, Sylvia. 1939. *African Women: A Study of the Ibo of Nigeria.* London: Faber and Faber.

Lévi-Strauss, Claude. 1976. *Structural Anthropology.* Vol. 2. Chicago: University of Chicago Press.

Levy-Bruhl, Lucien. 1923. *Primitive Mentality.* Lilian A. Clare, trans. New York: A. A. Knopf.

———. 1926. *How Natives Think.* Lilian A. Clare, trans. New York: Macmillan.

MacGregor, J. K. 1909. "Some Notes on Nsibidi." *Journal of the Royal Anthropological Institute* 39:209–19.

Maine, Henry S. 1870. *Ancient Law: Its Connection with the Early History of Society, and its Relation to Modern Ideas.* London: John Murray.

Malinowski, Bronislaw. 1922. *Argonauts of the Western Pacific.* New York: Dutton.

———. 1948. *Magic, Science and Religion and Other Essays.* Boston: Beacon Press.

Marcus, George, and Michael Fisher. 1986. *Anthropology as Cultural Critique: An Experimental Moment in the Human Sciences.* Chicago: University of Chicago Press.

Mauss, Marcel. 1973. "Techniques of the Body." *Economy and Society* 2 (1): 70–88.

Mba, Nina E. 1982. *Nigerian Women Mobilized: Women's Political Activity in Southern Nigeria, 1900–1965.* Berkeley: U. C. Institute of International Studies.

Mbiti, John. 1969. *African Religions and Philosophy.* London: Heinemann.

McCall, John C. 1992. *The Ohafia War Dance as Lived Experience: History and Identity in a Nigerian Community.* Ph.D. dissertation. Indiana University, Bloomington.

———. 1993a. "Dancing the Past: Experiencing Historical Knowledge in

Ohafia, Nigeria." *Passages: A Chronicle of the Humanities* (Evanston: Northwestern University) 4 (1): 8–9.

———. 1993b. "Making Peace with Agwu." *Anthropology and Humanism Quarterly* 18 (2): 56–66.

———. 1995. "Rethinking Ancestors in Africa." *Africa* 65 (2): 256–70.

———. 1996a. "Portrait of a Brave Woman." *American Anthropologist* 98 (1): 127–36.

———. 1996b. "Discovery as a Research Strategy." *Anthropology Newsletter* 37 (2): 44, 42.

Meek, Charles K. 1925. *The Northern Tribes of Nigeria.* London: Oxford University Press.

Mendosa, E. L. 1976. "Elders, Office-holders and Ancestors among the Sisala of Northern Ghana." *Africa* 46 (1): 57–60.

Merleau-Ponty, M. 1989. *Phenomenology of Perception.* London: Routledge.

Metuh, Efefie Ikenga. 1985. *African Religions in Western Conceptual Schemes: The Problem of Interpretation.* Ibadan: Claverianum Press.

Mmuko, Oke. 1991. 25-A-01. Recorded oration.

Morgan, 1877. *Ancient Society.* New York: Holt.

Mudimbe, V. Y. 1988. *The Invention of Africa.* Bloomington: Indiana University Press.

Ndukwe, Obuba. 1971. "The Age-Groups in Ibo-land." *Contributions to the Study of Ibo Society and Culture in Nigeria.* Prague: University of 17th November of Prague, Sborník studenstký ch practí, císlo 2.

Nietzsche, Friedrich. 1909. *The Will to Power: An Attempted Transvaluation of All Values.* New York: Macmillan.

Nketia, J. H. Kwabena. 1958. "Traditional Music of the Ga People." *African Music* 2 (1): 21–27.

Nsugbe, P. O. 1974. *Ohaffia: A Matrilineal Ibo People.* London: Oxford University Press.

Ntima, Agwu. 1990. 11-A-01. Recorded interview.

Nwabara, S. N. 1977. *Iboland: A Century of Contact with Britain, 1860–1960.* London: Hodder and Stoughton.

Nwoga, Donatus Ibe. 1984. *The Supreme God as Stranger in Igbo Religious Thought.* Imo State: Hawk Press.

Obbo, Christine. 1976. "Dominant Male Ideology and Female Options: Three East African Case Studies." *Africa* 46 (4): 371–89.

Obiego, Cosmas Okechukwu. 1984. *African Image of the Ultimate Reality: An Analysis of Igbo Ideas of Life and Death in Relation to Chukwu-God.* Frankfurt am Main: Peter Lang.

Oboler, Regina S. 1980. "Is the Female Husband a Man? Woman/Woman Marriage among the Nandi of Kenya." *Ethnology* 19 (1): 69–88.

O'Brien, Denise. 1977. "Female Husbands in African Societies." In A. Schlegel, ed., *Sexual Stratification: A Cross Cultural View.* New York: Columbia University Press.

Odachi, Okoro. 1965. Unpublished history of Akanu, Ohafia.

Ogbalu, F. Chidozie. 1981. *The Correct Way to Write Igbo.* Onitsha, Nigeria: University Publishing.

Ojiono, Udo. 1991. 23-A-01. Recorded interview.

Okorocha, Cyril C. 1987. *The Meaning of Religious Conversion in Africa: The Case of the Igbo of Nigeria*. Aldershot, England: Brookfield.

Omiko, Kalu. 1991. 30-B-01. Recorded interview.

Ortner, Sherry. 1984. "Theory in Anthropology since the 'Sixties." *Comparative Studies in Society and History* 26:126–66.

Ottenberg, Simon. 1968. *Double Descent in an African Society: The Afikpo Village Group*. Seattle: University of Washington Press.

———. 1989. *Boyhood Rituals in an African Society: An Interpretation*. Seattle: University of Washington Press.

Peek, Philip M. 1991. "Introduction." *African Divination Systems*. Bloomington: Indiana University Press.

Perham, Margery. 1962 (1937). *Native Administration in Nigeria*. London: Oxford University Press.

Prince, R. 1964. "Indigenous Yoruba Psychiatry." In A. Keiv, ed., *Magic, Faith and Healing: Studies in Primitive Psychiatry Today*. Glenco, IL: Free Press.

———. 1976. "Psychotherapy as the Manipulation of Endogenous Healing Mechanisms: A Transcultural Survey." *Transcultural Psychiatric Research Review* 13:115–33.

Rigby, P. 1968. "Some Gogo Rituals of 'Purification': An Essay on Social and Moral Categories." In E. Leach, ed., *Dialectic in Practical Religion*. Cambridge: Cambridge University Press.

Ritzenthaler, Robert E. 1960. "Anlu: A Women's Uprising in the British Cameroons." *African Studies* (Johannesburg) 19:151–56.

Rivière, P. G. 1971. "Marriage: A Reassessment." In R. Needham, ed., *Rethinking Kinship and Marriage*. London: Tavistock.

Rosaldo, Michelle. 1980. *Knowledge and Passion: Ilongot Notions of Self and Social Life*. Cambridge: Cambridge University Press.

Rosaldo, Renato. 1980. *Ilongot Headhunting, 1893–1974*. Stanford: Stanford University Press.

Rosen, Lawrence. 1979. "Social Identity and Points of Attachment: Approaches to Social Organization." In C. Geertz, H. Geertz, and L. Rosen, eds., *Meaning and Order in Moroccan Society*. London: Cambridge University Press.

Ruel, Malcolm. 1969. *Leopards and Leaders: Constitutional Politics among a Cross River People*. New York: Tavistock Publications.

Sartre, Jean-Paul. 1969. "Itinerary of a Thought." *New Left Review* 58: 43–66.

Schutz, Alfred. 1971. *The Problem of Social Reality*. Collected Papers, vol. 1, Maurice Natanson, ed. The Hague: Martinus Nijhoff.

Seligman, C. G., and B. Seligman. 1932. *Pagan Tribes of the Nilotic Sudan*. London: Routledge and Kegan Paul.

Shapiro, Warren. 1988. "Ritual Kinship, Ritual Incorporation and the Denial of Death." *Man* 23 (2): 275–97.

Skomal, Susan. 1995. "Science in Anthropology." *Anthropology Newsletter* 36 (7): 1, 5.

Spencer, Herbert. 1860. "The Social Organism." *Westminster Review* 17: 51–68.

———. 1885. *Principles of Sociology*. New York: Appleton-Century-Crofts.

Stayt, H. A. 1931. *The Bavenda*. London: Cass.

Stoller, Paul. 1989a. *The Taste of Ethnographic Things: The Senses in Anthropology*. Philadelphia: University of Pennsylvania Press.

———. 1989b. *Fusion of the Worlds: An Ethnography of Possession among the Songhay of Niger*. Chicago: University of Chicago Press.

———. 1997. *Sensuous Scholarship*. Philadelphia: University of Pennsylvania Press.

Stoller, Paul, and Cheryl Olkes. 1987. *In Sorcery's Shadow: A Memoir of Apprenticeship among the Songhay of Niger*. Chicago: University of Chicago Press.

Stone, Ruth. 1988. *Dried Millet Breaking*. Bloomington: Indiana University Press.

Strathern, A. 1979. " 'We Are All of One Father Here': Models of Descent in the New Guinea Highlands." In L. Holy, ed., *Segmentary Lineage Systems Reconsidered*. The Queen's University Papers in Social Anthropology, vol. 4. Belfast: Department of Social Anthropology, Queens University.

Talbot, P. Amaury. 1912. *In the Shadow of the Bush*. London: Heinemann.

———. 1932. *Tribes of the Niger Delta: Their Religions and Customs*. New York: Barnes and Noble.

Thomas, Northcote. 1914. *Anthropological Report on Ibo-Speaking Peoples of Nigeria, Part IV: Law and Custom of the Ibo of Asaba District, S. Nigeria*. London: Harrison and Sons.

Thompson, R. F. 1963. *African Art in Motion*. Los Angeles: University of California Press.

Thornton, Robert. 1980. *Space, Time, and Culture among the Iraqw of Tanzania*. New York: Academic Press.

Turino, Thomas. 1990. "Structure, Context and Strategy in Musical Ethnography." *Ethnomusicology* 34 (3): 399–412.

Turner, Edith. 1992. *Experiencing Ritual: A New Interpretation of African Healing*. Philadelphia: University of Pennsylvania Press.

Tylor, Edward B. 1873. *Primitive Culture*. New York: Harper Torchbook.

Uche, A. K. 1960. *Custom and Practice in Ohafia*. Aba, Nigeria: Research Institute of African Religions Press.

Uchendu, Victor C. 1965. *The Igbo of Southeast Nigeria*. New York: Holt Rinehart and Winston.

———. 1976. "Ancestorcide! Are African Ancestors Dead?" In W. H. Newell, ed., *Ancestors*. Paris: Mouton Publishers.

Ukwu, U. I. 1967. "The Development of Trade and Marketing in Igboland." *Journal of the Historical Society of Nigeria* 3 (4): 647–62.

Uma, Eze O. 1989. *Factors in Ohafia History*. Elu Ohafia, Nigeria: SKA Press.

Ume, Ajike Kalu. 1960. *Ohafia Dike n'Agha*. Calabar: Hope Waddell Press.

———. N.d. Unpublished history of Akanu, Ohafia.

Van Allen, Judith. 1972. "Sitting on a Man: Colonialism and the Lost

Political Institutions of Igbo Women." *Canadian Journal of African Studies* 6 (2): 168–81.

Van Leynseele, P. 1979. *Les Libinza de la Ngiri.* Ph.D. thesis. University of Leiden, The Netherlands.

Vansina, Jan. 1965. *Oral Tradition: A Study in Historical Methodology.* H. M. Wright, trans. Chicago: Aldine Publishing.

Vansina, Jan, Raymond Mauny, and L. V. Thomas, eds. 1964. *The Historian in Tropical Africa.* London: Oxford University Press.

White, Hayden. 1978. "The Burden of History." In H. White, ed., *Tropics of Discourse.* Baltimore: Johns Hopkins University Press.

Wiedner, Donald L. 1964. *A History of Africa South of the Sahara.* New York: Vintage Books.

Wilson, Peter J. 1967. "Status Ambiguity and Spirit Possession." *Man,* n.s., 2:366–78.

# Index

Aba, *dibịa* market in, 24
Abam, 82, 89, 107, 171n. 8; common ancestry with Ohafia, 170n. 4
Abiriba, 107, 108, 111
Achebe, Chinua, 115, 146
Achebe, Chinwe, 145–46
Afigbo, A. E., 82
Afikpo, 87, 138, 169n. 2
Agara, Joseph, 26, 54, 57–58, 59, 165n. 5
age-grades, 36, 79–80, 93; obligations to, 31–32, 89–90, 91, 107
age-sets, 30, 123, 136, 173n. 2
Agwu, 30, 50, 165n. 4, 174n. 2; shrines to, 30, 32–33, 38, 40, 43–44, 142–43, 144
Akanu (Ohafia), 34, 91, 108; founding of, 153–60; tutelary deity of, 123. *See also* Amafor quarter; Ekelogo quarter; Ndi Odo quarter; Utugokoko quarter
Akwette, 171n. 8
*alụsi. See arụnsi*
Amaekpu (Ohafia), 108
Amafor quarter (Akanu), 154, 155, 156
American Anthropological Association, debate over science in anthropology and, 11
ancestors, 21, 158; academic debates about, 97–113, 172nn. 1, 2; appeals to, 124, 128, 131; communicate through dreams, 26; dance and, 16, 62, 63, 172n. 3; libations offered to, 32, 48, 75–76, 103, 144; Ohafia term for, 173n. 8; prenatal agreements and, 130, 151
Aniakor, Chike, 115
Appiah, Kwame A., 8, 164n. 5

Archives of Traditional Music, 175n. 7, 177
Aro, 54, 107; British and, 84–88, 171n. 8; Ohafia and, 82–83, 166n. 6
Arochukwu, 88, 107
Arua, A. O., 86–87, 88
*arụnsi*, 140. *See also* shrines
Asaga (Ohafia), 126
Atulị Abalị. *See* Night Society
Awkuzu, 83–84
Aworinde, Awotunde, 175n. 7
Azande, 150
Azuonye, Chukwuma, 54, 59, 92, 119, 161, 163n. 3

Bantu, southern, female husbands among, 132
Bascom, William, 148, 175n. 7
Ben-Amos, Paula, 69
Bende, 86, 155
Beng, 172n. 2
Biafran war, 55, 94–95, 172n. 18
birth control, 174n. 8
black, significance of, 30
Boas, Franz, 9, 10
Brain, James L., 98
brave women, 117, 126; head-taking and, 118, 119–20. *See also* Nne Uko Uma Awa
bride wealth, 174n. 9
British. *See* colonial period
burial, 76–77; of chief, 31, 53–54, 66, 79; of king, 79, 167n. 22; of Nna Nduka, 34–37; second, 34, 35, 37; subfloor, 103, 110, 175n. 4; trophy heads and, 92; of umbilical cord, 102; war dance and, 3, 8; of women, 103